Hold the Line, Please

Please

Memoirs of a P&O Ship's Telephonist

Freda Bassindale

Bassman Books

Published by Bassman Books, Burnside Cottage,
Newhall, Balblair, Dingwall, IV7 8LT

First published in 2021

A catalogue record for this book is available from the
British Library

ISBN 978-0-9956440-6-9

Printed by J Thomson, The Green House,
Beechwood Business Park North, Inverness, IV2 3BL

Set in Palatino 11/13pt

This book is dedicated to Alison Ross, a fellow Scot and good friend.

We sailed together on board P&O passenger liners *SS Iberia* and *SS Orsova* where Alison was the senior nursing sister. As a crew member, not of officer rank, my movements on board ship were restricted, but Alison's friendship opened doors for me and enabled me to mix, fairly freely, with officers and passengers. This made my time at sea much more enjoyable than it could have been.

Contents

Prologue

How it all began

It was a crisp November day when I arrived at Tilbury Docks to join the *SS Iberia*, at 29,614 tons the fourth largest and, with a speed of thirty-four knots, one of the fastest ships in the P&O fleet at that time. We were heading for Australia via South Africa. The ship was then to spend five months cruising in the Pacific, returning to the UK via South Africa, a total journey of seven-and-a-half months.

Two incidents in my life had brought me to this point. When I was eighteen and working as a telephonist in Inverness Telephone Exchange, I connected a person-to-person call for a lady who told me that she was arranging an interview with the Lady Superintendent at the Cunard Shipping Line, for a post as ship's telephonist. While I made the long, complicated connection, she told me about her plans for a life at sea. I liked the sound of it all and decided that one day I would do the same.

The second incident occurred when I was a serving policewoman in Edinburgh City Police. I'd been seconded to the Criminal Investigation Department (CID). Eight women shared a small office, and one morning we were sitting at our desks awaiting the day's assignments. Our Officer-in-Charge had just delivered a stinging rebuke, having caught us out in a practice which, although strictly against the rules, we indulged in regularly. We just hadn't been caught before.

In the 1960s, prior to the Sex Discrimination Act 1975, policewomen dealt with women's matters. Rape, incest, indecent assault, domestic abuse, missing persons and shoplifters were the crimes we responded to. When a shoplifter was apprehended, all items stolen by that person were carefully noted in the arresting officer's notebook, and the article placed in a plastic production bag. This was sealed and labelled, showing the type of article, name of accused, date apprehended and arresting officer's details. The bag was then stored in a cupboard in the women detectives' office awaiting delivery to court for the ensuing trial or for return to the owner if the accused pleaded guilty. Occasionally, when our duties kept us at our desks over mealtimes, we borrowed from the stock of productions: a bag of crisps, a bar of chocolate, a bottle of lemonade, always making sure these items were replaced as soon as possible. Now someone had slipped up and a production was missing. We had been given a severe dressing down.

After two years in the CID, my enthusiasm was beginning to pall. The women I worked with were all very pleasant and I got on well with them, but they had become as hard as nails. Nothing moved them. A rape victim was accorded as much sympathy as a woman who had had her purse pinched. The women discussed cases in graphic detail using the coarsest of language, and I realised it was all in a day's work for them and they slept easy in their beds at night. I was made of softer stuff and had nightmares. I now remembered the lady whose call to Cunard I had connected all those years ago, and I thought it was time I did something about it. I sat down there and then and typed letters of application to P&O, Cunard and Shaw Saville for work as a telephonist on board ship. The replies from Cunard and Shaw Saville said that their waiting lists were very long, but P&O agreed to put me on their list.

Eighteen months later, three days before I was due to start a thirteen-day holiday cruise on board the P&O liner *SS Chusan*, a letter arrived from P&O asking me to attend for interview at their London Headquarters. One week after the end of my holiday, I travelled to London, had a successful interview and resigned from the Police. I had served seven years and five months and I had no regrets. I celebrated in style with a "do" at the RAF Club in Abercrombie Place, Edinburgh and so began the next chapter in my career.

Part 1

Pacific Cruising

Tilbury to Sydney, Sydney to Tilbury
November 1968 to May 1969

In the early evening of 13th November 1968, *SS Iberia* edged her way out of the dock at Tilbury and headed down the Thames. As I stood on deck, watching the land receding into the distance, I experienced my first feelings of homesickness, feelings that were to plague me for all of my seagoing days.

My work colleagues were Rosemary, who shared a cabin with me, Rose and our supervisor, Norma. Norma was a small, wiry Liverpudlian with a wicked sense of humour and bow legs, the result of her poor diet during the war, she told me. Rose had a Scots boyfriend, Tom, who hailed from Fife, and by the time the trip was over, Rose was two weeks away from giving birth, an event kept secret from the entire ship's company bar the doctor, for the seven-and-a-half months of the voyage.

The telephonists' quarters were on E Deck aft, in a small alley-way beside the Tourist Class passenger cabins. We shared the alleyway with four stewardesses and ate in the tourist restaurant, where a table was reserved for our use. We had waiter service and ate from the same menu as the passengers. For the entire trip I was to work every day without a day off. This may sound extreme, but with four girls in the Telephone Exchange, we worked shifts: 1: 6.30-9am and 4.30-7.30pm; 2: 9am-12noon; 3: 12noon-4.30pm and 7.30-midnight; 4: midnight to 6am. The busy time was between midnight and 1am when the passengers returned to their cabins and began ordering tea and toast, or cocoa, or Horlicks. When things quietened down, I got out the deckchair, pillows and blankets that were kept in a cupboard in the telephone exchange and bedded down for the night. The door to the exchange was locked, the blind pulled down on the porthole and the night buzzer activated. I usually managed to get a few hours' sleep on night shift. This was a normal occurrence on all the P&O ships. It was common knowledge that it went on, but as long as nothing drastic happened, a blind eye was turned.

The telephone exchange was pretty small: about 3x3 metres and it held a two-position switchboard of the type used in all GPO telephone exchanges. This meant a board containing rows of apertures with a light above and the number of the extension below. On the desk were two rows of cords for connecting the callers and a row of switches which were pushed forward to speak and back to ring the number called. When a call came in, the light was illuminated, and to answer the call one of the cords was plugged into the appropriate aperture. The second cord was plugged into the extension called.

While we were at sea the only calls we dealt with were internal: passengers and officers calling one another or calls between departments. When we reached port, landlines were connected to the ship and external calls were possible.

At sea, contact from ship-to-shore was made via the Radio Department which had several radio officers. Nowadays this department no longer exists, nor are there any telephonists employed on board. The telephone system for internal calls is fully automated and ship-to-shore communications changed with the arrival of satellite technology. There is now an e-mail system for passengers and crew to use and mobile phones can be used if the ship is within range of a shore station. An Electro-Technical Officer or Computer Officer deals with repairs and operating problems.

I had had a taste of the good life on board a P&O liner when I joined SS *Chusan* for a thirteen-day cruise in 1967 and again in 1968. My three friends and I had enjoyed the many parties we were invited to, both in the public rooms and in the cabins of the

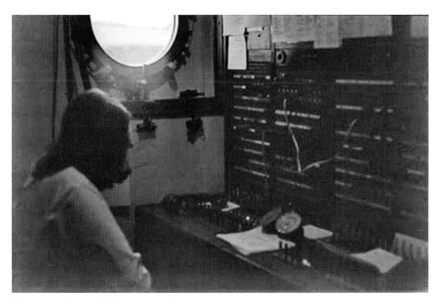

Rita, senior telephonist on Orsova.

deck officers and engineers. The officers were always charming and looked so handsome in their dress uniforms, that our heads were turned by all the attention heaped upon us. I foolishly expected this to continue when I joined as a member of the ship's company, so you can imagine my disappointment when I discovered that I had the rank of Leading Hand: well below the rank of officer and just a teeny-weeny bit above the rank of crew member. On my induction tour of the ship, the Senior Telephonist stressed that I was not allowed to use the public rooms or to mingle with passengers. Mixing with officer ranks was definitely prohibited and if I failed to follow the company rules I was liable to be disciplined or even sacked. I looked forward to a miserable existence on board.

During my first spell on duty, I made a loudspeaker announcement and immediately got a call from the surgery.

"What part of Scotland are you from, then?" This was Alison, the Senior Nursing Sister who became a good friend. She was my entry into the social scene of the officer class, when she invited me to parties in her cabin where I met her fellow officers. I'm not sure that any of the officers realised that I was breaking company rules and I had no intention of enlightening them. To be invited to parties and gatherings in the officers' cabins was a vast improvement to my on-board social life and I never turned down a party invitation except in exceptional circumstances.

Down below, the crew were a mixed lot. The stokers and winchmen were the most rough and ready bunch I'd ever seen. The waiting staff and the bedroom stewards were mostly homosexual.

In the late sixties, Australia was still taking migrants from both Britain and Holland, and Iberia passengers consisted mainly of migrant families. In 1947 the Government of Australia initiated the Assisted Passage Migration Scheme whereby adults from Britain were able to travel to Australia for £10 a head. Children could travel free. The country desperately needed white British stock to increase its population, sadly depleted by the war, and to build its burgeoning economy. The migrants were promised jobs, housing and a good lifestyle and many thousands responded to the call. Labelled "Ten Pound Poms," those able to take advantage of the scheme were limited to white British citizens. At the time, Australia operated a White Australia Policy and this meant that blacks and Asians were not accepted into the country. During the period of the migration scheme, 1947 to 1982, it is estimated that one and a half million Brits took advantage to travel to the other side of the world in search of a better life.

In 1966 Australia introduced a wider immigration policy whereby migrants were accepted for their suitability as settlers, their ability to integrate and the possession of qualifications useful to Australia. This heralded the end of the White Australia Policy.

Our first stop after London was Rotterdam, where we embarked several hundred Dutch nationals on their way to a new life in either South Africa or Australia. With a full load of families on board, life was anything but dull. The telephone exchange was the first port of call for all enquiries, so the telephonists were a mine of information and privy to everything that occurred on board.

Iberia had the reputation of being a jinxed ship and this trip was no exception. Four days after leaving Tilbury, we entered the Bay of Biscay, when at 10 o'clock at night we suffered a major engine failure and were left without heating and lighting. We also had no water. The ship sailed along very slowly and we took three days to

Iberia medical staff, left to right: Ross, hospital attendant; Dora Anderson, nursing sister; David Holroyd, junior surgeon; Mike Cowen, senior surgeon; Alison Ross, senior nursing sister; Jack Last, pharmacist.

navigate the Bay of Biscay. On our way down the west coast of Africa, a generator broke down and the air conditioning went off. The engineers' department worked many long hours to try to fix it.

On Tuesday 19th November I wrote to my mother, "At the moment we're limping along in the direction of Dakar with the engines on the verge of conking out and doing the grand old speed of about six knots. The engines broke down twice during the night and it seems there's something drastically wrong and we're going to have to spend three days in Dakar to have them repaired."

We crawled into Dakar, the capital of Senegal and instead of staying there for a few hours we were there for two days. My first taste of Africa was also my first sight of grinding poverty. I went ashore with Rose and we picked our way gingerly between the potholes of the dusty road that was the main thoroughfare between the port and the town centre. Large trees bordered the road and were perfect cover from the searing heat of the African sun. Under every inch of shade sat a hotch-potch of humanity: spindly limbs, glazed eyes, runny noses. Those that were clad wore tattered bits and pieces, barely covering the emaciated bodies underneath. Mangy dogs and snotty-nosed children played noisily on the road. The people were very friendly however, and it never entered my head that I might be assaulted or robbed. I walked from the ship to the centre of the town several times and never came to any harm.

There was little traffic around, mainly run-down lorries held together by string and wire. In 1968 Dakar was a busy town with a population of about 400,000. The harbour was full of large ships: liners such as the one Rose and I had just left and mega-tankers of the massive Maru Line, flying the Japanese rising sun.

Rose and I were heading for the Medina Market in the African quarter of the town. Our mission was to buy a parrot! I shudder with shame now when I think of it, but in 1968 we were not aware of the probably not-then-illegal trade in wildlife and the purchase of a parrot in an African market seemed to me to be perfectly normal.

Open both night and day the market was worth our long trek. The market place was big and busy, and large elegant ladies dressed in dazzling turbans and kaftans, crowded round the heavily laden stalls. Mounds of brightly coloured fruits and vegetables I'd never seen before and couldn't identify, shared their space with spices as colourful as the customers' attire, and assaulted the senses with their pungent smells. It was also very noisy. Bargaining was the order of the day, and deals were struck loudly and quickly. I watched one deal concluded satisfactorily, and a large lady sailed past me with a magnificent look of triumph on her face. It was fascinating to watch and I would have spent all day there, but we had a job to do: track down a parrot.

It wasn't difficult to find the bird section: we followed the noise. There were rows and rows of cages containing birds of every size and hue. Multi-coloured finches sang merrily, completely ignorant of their fate; jewel-coloured parrots and parakeets squawked and screeched and fought battles with each other when their space was

Dakar road scene.

in danger of being invaded. Little animals, caught in the wild and intended for consumption, were crammed into cages too small for comfort. I couldn't bear to look. Snakes and lizards, prized for their uses in medicine I was told, slithered into any available shade away from the searing heat of the sun. It was a sorry sight. Rose and I were also attracting attention as we were the only white people there. The native market was definitely not one of the sights on the tourist itinerary for our ship.

At the parrot stand, we chose a fine specimen, together with a wicker cage, and after some half-hearted haggling, made our purchase. This parrot at least, would have a fairly good life as it was destined for the cabin of the ship's bo'sun, Tom. Named Rover, this lively parrot learned to speak and whistle and was allowed to fly freely in the confines of the cabin. He was well fed and pampered.

We weren't the only ones buying a parrot that day. As we left the market, we bumped into Rod, one of the ship's engineers on his way to buy three parrots for himself and his mates. We helped him carry them back to the ship.

Apart from the poverty, there was another side to Dakar and I had a chance to sample it next day when I went on an organised trip to the impressive Presidential Palace with its exotic gardens, strutting cranes and ebony-faced guards in scarlet uniform. We watched a display of African dancing and singing and sampled exotic fruits. The passengers loved this.

My abiding memory of Dakar, however, is one of smell. Dakar's main production at the time was groundnuts and there were several processing factories in the city. The smell was something between a warm macaroon biscuit and a soft perfume. It was not unpleasant, if a little sickly.

At the beginning of the 19th century, Dakar was a small fishing village at the southern end of the Cape Verde peninsula. In 1849 the first groundnuts were exported from the area, an activity that continued while I was there in 1968. By improving the port facilities and extending the railway through the heart of the peanut-growing area, Dakar became the most important port on the west coast of Africa, and in August 1960 the city became the capital of the Independent Republic of Senegal.

According to Wikipedia, the estimated population of the city of Dakar in 2013 was 1,146,053 and it is described as a major financial centre, home to several national and regional banks and many international organisations, NGOs and international research centres. Between 1978 and 2007 Dakar was the finishing point of the Paris to Dakar Rally, an event that brought worldwide attention to the poverty of Dakar and Senegal.

As we neared the equator, plans were made for the "Crossing the Line" ceremony. Passengers and crew members crossing the equator for the first time were brought before King Neptune who sat on his throne and accused them of various dastardly deeds. Neptune's assistants then plastered each one in tomato sauce, flour and other gunge and finally threw them into the swimming pool. Neptune was also assisted by two nymphs who sat by his side and shouted encouragement when he was being too soft on the participants. Norma and I took on that job. It was great fun and the passengers loved it. As it was my first crossing of the equator, I too got the treatment.

I was not allowed on deck to socialise with passengers or officers but I now found a way to get round this rule. I volunteered to

Rose and Freda with parrots.

take part in the various theme nights held on board for the passengers. The first of these was Country Fair where the ballroom was set up to look like a fairground with coconut shies, roll-the-penny, hoop-la, and loud music. I helped out on the "Charley's Face" stall where players had to kick a football into the mouth of a clown to win a prize.

After the entertainment I was allowed to join the other participants in one of the public bars for a celebratory drink. It was a start, and my initial disappointment faded when I realised that it was possible for me to enjoy life on board. As first and second class passengers were separated in 1968, the entertainment was repeated the following evening, giving me two occasions to socialise. With careful planning, I could circumvent the rules without jeopardising my position.

Sailing in the South Atlantic I saw during the day, my first flying fish, and during the evening, my first sight of phosphorescence. Flying fish are torpedo shaped, enabling them to gather enough speed to break the surface, while their pectoral fins and forked tails get them airborne. They can sometimes reach a height of four feet and travel a distance of up to six hundred feet, an action probably developed to enable them to escape predators.

Phosphorescence of the sea, which was something I found wonderful to watch, is caused by the presence of blooming phytoplankton. Standing on the stern of the ship, I watched the water churned up by the propellers, glowing eerily in the darkness. I spent a lot of time on deck. I had approached the Purser's Department and discovered that the telephonists were allowed access to the Tourist Class decks as long as they kept a low profile. Once again my luck was in.

It was in Cape Town that I had my first taste of apartheid. We had on board a young Dutchman and his Fijian wife who were migrating to Australia. They were a popular couple and mixed well with their fellow passengers. When we reached Cape Town however, the authorities forbade the couple to go ashore together. They could go ashore singly, but not as a couple. If they refused to comply, they were told they would be kept under lock and key until the ship sailed. They chose to stay on board.

Cape Town was a lovely city and at that time very safe. As we sailed into port I couldn't take my eyes off the view. Table Mountain was in full ceremonial dress: her tablecloth of white fluffy cloud draped dramatically over the top.

The crew had been given advice on apartheid before going ashore, but the reality was a shock and took some getting used to. There were separate railway stations, Post Offices and even banks for black and white. I went ashore with Norma. Norma was small and dark-haired with a complexion verging on caramel. When she ventured into a public toilet signposted Net Blankes, nobody checked her as they thought she was coloured. Only when she was coming out and met a black person going in did she realise her mistake.

It was hard sometimes to distinguish between black and white. The Cape Coloured people weren't really black, in fact many of them looked quite white, but they had been categorised as black by the Government and had to use the black facilities.

Norma and I took the cable-car to the top of Table Mountain. It was a hair-raising ride, but the view from the top was magnificent. To the north, the coast of Africa stretched into infinity, while below Table Mountain, Cape Town sprawled in urban splendour. Away

Cape Town from Table Mountain.

to the east I could see huge mountain ranges, all blue and red, stretching for many miles.

We walked everywhere. The city squares were perfect for people-watching. The wonderful Botanical Gardens on Government Avenue were a haven of peace. The harbour area however, bustled with activity. The railway lines to the docks carried many huge, beautiful old steam trains, puffing and chuffing and hissing contentedly, still lovingly tended by people who appreciated their beauty. They ferried coal and other goods to the port for shipment all over the world. That evening I went on a City Lights tour. I don't remember where else we went, but I do remember the drive up Signal Hill where we viewed the whole of Cape Town sparkling below. When Iberia sailed at ten o'clock that evening, Table Mountain was illuminated in our honour and it was a spectacular sight.

Durban was, in the sixties, also a lovely city with beautiful parks and several miles of gently shelving beaches where the rolling combers of the Indian Ocean broke relentlessly on golden sands. I spent a hot sunny afternoon on the beach, marred only by the sight of separate sections for white and coloured people.

As I walked through a park, some white children played on swings. Nearby, a coloured couple with a child of about four sat on a bench. The little girl was pleading with her mother to let her play on the swings and it was heart-breaking to hear the mother try to explain that because of her colour she wasn't allowed to.

Travelling across the Indian Ocean in the sixties took ten days. Whenever I finished my shift at six o'clock in the morning, or before I went on duty at six, I went up on deck for some fresh air and to watch the sun rise. I loved to stand at the ship's rail, alone but for one or two of the Goanese crew sluicing down the deck.

Although we referred to the entire Indian crew as Goanese, strictly speaking they were not all from that part of India. According to P&O's history site, the Deck Ratings were Hindu or Moslem and were recruited from the various fishing communities in India, while the Engine Room Ratings were Pathan hill farmers from the area that is now Pakistan. The Catering Ratings were however, recruited from the Portuguese colony of Goa and were of the Christian faith. This meant they were happy to handle pork and beef, which the Hindu and Moslem crews disliked.

It was in 1842 that P&O positioned their first ship east of Suez and established a base in Calcutta. A service for passengers and freight was introduced between Calcutta and Suez, where an over-land journey to Alexandria connected with another ship taking them to the UK. British officers and crew had to be relieved every two years and this was a costly business. Although officers were still replaced from the UK, it seemed sensible to recruit local Indian crews. Several manning strategies were applied, and in 1853 when P&O opened an office in Bombay, a manning structure was put in place that was to endure for over a hundred years.

On this particular journey across the Indian Ocean we were accompanied for several days by an albatross. Every morning when I went on deck there he was, gliding effortlessly and sound-lessly alongside the stern of the ship. If there was no-one about, I talked to him. I asked him where he was bound, where was he born, how old was he? Did he ever get tired? He never answered, but we did make regular eye contact. The bird's wing span was about six or seven feet and I noted in my diary that he didn't move his wings once all the time I watched him. As soon as the passengers ventured on deck, he disappeared only to re-appear during the night to continue his journey.

Standing on an empty deck at night was another pastime of mine. In 1968 the ship didn't thunder along between ports during the night, and the soft throb of the engines, the gentle noise of the waves slapping against the side of the ship gave me a sense of peace and comfort. The southern sky, a vast black, velvet backcloth to the millions of twinkling stars, never failed to enthral. The great Southern Cross, the only constellation in the southern hemisphere I could identify with confidence, dominated the sky. Shooting stars abounded and lasted for several seconds. It was as if a great stellar strobe show had been put on for my benefit.

Occasionally the lights of a distant ship came into view. I often wondered where it was bound and if there was someone standing on the deck just like me, looking at us and thinking similar thoughts.

I was excited about visiting Australia, but it was unfortunate that Perth was the first city on our itinerary. Perth was flat and, so my diary says, populated by bungalows. Our ship berthed at the port of Fremantle, an altogether more interesting city, and I would have been better served had I stayed there. Instead I went on a guided tour of Perth. I didn't see anything that grabbed my attention, nor did the bus stop at any of the sites we visited. Our lacklustre guide didn't inspire us as he intoned "this is a sugar factory" "that is a statue to…" "that is a hospital." I cheered up however, when we sailed from Fremantle later that evening. We were given a rousing send-off by hundreds of cheering residents and a pipe band!

Adelaide, our next stop, made me feel I was back in Edinburgh. The lovely old buildings and churches were very familiar. The streets were wide and tree-lined and the whole city was surrounded by parks. From the centre of the town you could see the beautiful hills of the Mount Lofty Range in the distance. There was a two-mile walk from the ship to the city centre, and for most of the way the road wound through flat grassland, before coming suddenly to the outskirts of the city. I spent my few hours ashore just wandering through the parks and sitting at an outdoor café drinking coffee and watching the world go by.

I stood on deck later that afternoon watching one of the Goanese deck crew try to land a giant stingray which he had caught on his fishing line. After about an hour he managed to land the still-struggling fish on to the deck. It weighed over 200lbs and caused quite a stir on the ship and at the quayside. I would have preferred it to have escaped the hook, but I was told the Goanese crew would be dining well for the next day or two.

My first visit to the city of Melbourne was one I'll never forget. Melbourne Harbour sits in the centre of a huge semi-circular bay with the city stretching from one end to the other. It was early evening and just beginning to get dark. Iberia was travelling slowly towards the distant pier, when suddenly we were in the middle of an electric storm. Great flashes of lightning lit up the entire bay. Dozens of branched strobes zig-zagged rapidly across the sky as far as the eye could see. It was a wondrous sight and the decks of the ship were crowded with passengers and crew alike, marvelling at nature's spectacular show, which continued for the best part of an hour.

Melbourne is now the second largest city in Australia. It was founded in 1835 and declared a city by Queen Victoria in 1847. Looking at contemporary pictures of Melbourne, I can't see anything that reminds me of the city I visited in 1968. Perhaps my memory has let me down, but I'm sure trams trundled through the city centre: a centre that comprised beautiful buildings no more than a couple of storeys high, a city with an old-fashioned feel to it.

Sailing through The Heads into Sydney Harbour was a wonderful experience. Hundreds of small craft sailed alongside, their occupants shouting greetings to all on board and providing a colourful escort for our great white liner as she glided up the bay to our berth at Circular Quay. There, hundreds lined the quay and packed into the terminal building, waiting for friends and relatives, or just to welcome our arrival.

When we docked in Sydney after our six weeks' voyage, a crew member was taken to hospital and found to be suffering from tuberculosis. When we next arrived in Sydney two weeks later, a mobile mass X-ray unit was waiting on the quay and every member of the crew, from the Captain downwards, was given a chest x-ray.

Scots always welcome fellow Scots wherever they are in the world, and Sydney was no exception. On my first visit there, I was on duty at the telephone exchange early in the morning after our arrival the night before. An elderly gentleman came on board selling newspapers and came to speak to me. He told me he came from the borders of Scotland and had been in Australia for nearly fifty years, but his Scots accent was as strong as if he'd only just arrived. I can't remember his name, but every time we docked in Sydney there he'd be, round for a blether and to present me with my free newspaper.

We had four days in Sydney before embarking on a series of Pacific cruises. I spent my time wandering round the city and enjoying the sunshine. Out strolling one evening, I heard the skirl of bagpipes. Following the sound, I came to a cinema where the red carpet had been laid out to welcome Sean Connery and his then wife, Diane Cilento, who were attending a film premiere. A huge crowd enjoyed the spectacle of a pipe band in full regalia, strutting their stuff. When the stars arrived they were very gracious, stopping to pose for the bank of photographers and chatting to some of the crowd.

Cruising in the southern hemisphere was a wonderful experience, although my first taste of Ozzy cruising was not what I expected. *Iberia* sailed from Sydney a few days before Christmas, on a cruise to New Zealand. It all started quietly enough and the Officers and Crew, who had formed a choir to sing carols on Christmas Eve, had no inkling of what was to come as we entertained the passengers in both the first class and tourist sections of the ship.

Nowadays, cruisers are usually elderly, but in the sixties many young Australians enjoyed cruising and they were a lively bunch. They liked their tinnies (beer) and consumed these in great numbers. When I went on duty at midnight on the 25th, *Iberia* was a battlefield. Christmas Day had been spent partying and no-one wanted to go to bed. Marauding gangs of prime Australian youth roamed the ship, tossing deckchairs overboard, overturning tables, knocking on doors and being a complete nuisance.

Below decks in the crew quarters, things were also a bit hectic. There were battles-royal everywhere, with several calls for the doctors to attend to crew members suffering various injuries, one being knife wounds. There was blood all over the Telephone Exchange as this was the first place the casualties came to for help. The Master at Arms and his hastily arranged posse were kept busy throughout the night. No sleeping on duty for me either.

On Boxing Day we anchored off Picton, New Zealand, a small village situated near the head of Queen Charlotte Sound on South Island. It was completely surrounded by hills and the only way out appeared to be by boat, of which there were hundreds. Norma and I were walking along the beach when we were approached by a young man in a yacht who asked us if we wanted to go for a sail. We did, and spent a good hour sailing round the bay.

I always made sure I saw as much as I could of the countries I visited, even if it was simply a trip into the port of call. I discovered that crew members could volunteer to act as "courier" on the ship's organised tours. All that was required of the courier was to assist the local guide in shepherding the passengers ashore and ensuring that the same number returned to the ship as had left it. Also, if there were places available on the tours, crew members could book a place at a special crew rate. There was also, at least once on each long trip, a crew sightseeing tour, so there were plenty of opportunities to see the places we visited. My favourite way of sightseeing however, was by way of local transport, which in most places was very cheap.

Wellington wasn't very big in 1968. I had most of the day off and decided to go on a bus tour of the city and its surrounds. We stopped off at a view point high above the city where we could see that the town was built into the hillsides. The many-coloured roofs of the houses and the green of the hills were quite a sight.

In the bay we could see the remains of the vehicle ferry *Wahine*, which had sunk nine months previously. In the early hours of the morning of 10th April 1968 the inter-island ferry foundered on the Barratt Reef at the entrance to Wellington Harbour. The ferry was crossing the Cook Strait en-route to Wellington from Lyttelton, when she encountered Cyclone Giselle which had already caused havoc in the North Island and was now heading south. Another storm had driven up the west coast of the South Island from Antarctica, and the two storms merged over Wellington. The resulting 170 miles-an-hour winds ripped off the roofs of nearly a hundred houses in Wellington.

With rising winds and heavy seas, the *Wahine* lost her radar, and a huge wave pushed her off course and in line with the Barratt Reef. The captain tried to turn the ship round to return to the open sea, but couldn't do so and the Wahine was driven on to the reef and grounded.

The order was given to abandon ship, but only four lifeboats could be launched. One lifeboat was swamped immediately. By midday, many people had come to the shore to watch the drama being played out at the harbour. Most of the ship's lifeboats were overturned, but some of the passengers were able to reach the rescue boats which surrounded the stricken ship. In total, 51 people drowned and two died of injuries later; 566 passengers were saved along with 110 crew. Six were posted missing. This event was still fresh in the minds of the people of Wellington and it was a sombre group that stood on the hill and listened to the tour guide relating the events of the sinking.

As I stood chatting to my friends, a woman approached me. "You sound Scottish. Where are you from?" she asked. I said Edinburgh (few people know where my home village of Rosemarkie is) and she started to cry. It turned out she had emigrated from Galashiels two years before and was desperately unhappy in New Zealand. Her husband loved the country and refused to go back to Scotland. I knew Galashiels quite well and we had a friendly chat about it. I often wondered if she got home to Gala or did she eventually learn to love New Zealand.

Next day we anchored in the Bay of Islands, midway between the villages of Waitangi and Russell. The ship's launches were kept busy all day as they ferried passengers and crew to both destinations.

Waitangi was where the New Zealand founding document, the Treaty of Waitangi was signed on 6th February 1840. The treaty, drafted by the newly-appointed first Governor of New Zealand William Hobson, and James Busby, the British Resident at Waitangi, was signed by the Governor on behalf of Queen Victoria, and over forty native Maori Chiefs. This treaty gave Britain sovereignty over New Zealand and gave the Maori people the rights of British Subjects.

In 1832 when James Busby was appointed British Resident at Waitangi, he was sent there partly because some of the Maori chiefs had petitioned the King asking for protection from the outrages of British subjects, many of them escaped convicts from Australia or deserters from ships, and from the French who, the Maori chiefs believed, were planning to annexe the country. Busby was given little support however, and had no means of enforcing his authority.

After a long Royal Navy career in which he saw action in the Napoleonic Wars and was twice captured by pirates, William Hobson was appointed New Zealand's first Governor in 1840. He landed at the Bay of Islands on 30th January that year, where he read his proclamation of appointment and met with James Busby. One week later the treaty was signed.

New Zealand now ceased to be a protectorate of New South Wales and became a colony in its own right, with Hobson as Governor, and Auckland as its capital city. The colony was not without its problems however, and there were frequent spats with settlers who wanted land and control of the administration of the colony. After barely two years as Governor, William Hobson died from a stroke at the age of forty-nine. Treaty House, the old residence of James Busby, had been turned into a museum, but visitors were few the day my friends and I visited, and we had the place almost to ourselves.

On Hogmanay there was a ring-in ceremony on the fo'c's'le of the ship where the crew gathered to ring a bell at midnight and sing Auld Lang Syne. The Scots on board were there in force and got a bit maudlin, singing as many Scots songs as we could remember, and sharing New Year bottles with all and sundry.

New Year's Day in Sydney was just another day, so some friends and I went off to Sydney Zoo for the afternoon. After a couple of hours there, we took a bus to Balmoral Bay and sat on the beach. I noticed three blocks of flats called Banchory, Ballater and Braemar. Cue: another bout of homesickness.

Our second cruise from Sydney began on 2nd January and consisted of mainly elderly passengers. The ship was only half full so we were looking forward to a quiet cruise after the terror of the previous one. Melbourne was our first port but I was keeping a low profile, as just after we sailed from Sydney, I crunched a tooth on a piece of Christmas cake and was in a lot of pain. Unfortunately it was Saturday when we were in Melbourne and there were no dental surgeries open, so I had to wait until we reached Auckland to get the tooth attended to.

I decided to have the tooth extracted as the company paid for it. If I'd had a filling I would have had to pay for it myself and I had better things to spend my money on, I decided. The dentist I visited was a big strapping fellow dressed in shorts and sandals and looked as if he would have no bother at all pulling my tooth. How wrong I was. He tugged and tugged, while the dental nurse struggled to hold me down on the chair. He had to stop half way through the extraction to apologise, before taking another few tugs and successfully pulling the tooth. No wonder he had difficulty: the tooth had a large, perfectly healthy hooked root.

Suva, the capital of Fiji, became one of my favourite ports and the memory of my first visit there remains clear. It was early in the morning and it had been raining heavily during the night. A wispy mist was rising from the luscious greenery covering the island. The air was soft and sweet and as we drew near to our berth, the gentle throb of the ship's engines was drowned out by the noise of the welcoming band and the excitement of the colourful crowds waiting on the quay.

No matter what time of day or night we arrived, the brass band of either the Fijian Police or the Army would be waiting to play us into port. Dressed in sparkling white sulus, the native skirts worn by Fijian men and women, with navy tunics for the Police and red tunics for the Army, these statuesque, handsome men were an amazing sight as they marched along the pier, performing sharp turns and quick manoeuvres for about half an hour.

I bought a local newspaper and on the front page was a picture of eight policewomen, looking very smart in their white sulus, blue shirts, white belts, shoes and ankle socks. These women were the first ever female recruits into the Fiji police.

There was always a local market set up just outside the pier selling anything you would care to buy: locally-made jewellery fashioned from shells and seeds; wood carvings, bowls, baskets and coral all beautifully painted. Next door, the food market had the weirdest-looking fruits and vegetables I had ever seen, including great sticks of green bananas, melons and paw-paw. They also sold live crabs, oysters and crayfish. As Suva was a "free" port and any goods bought were tax-free, It was a favourite place for the crew in particular, to buy cameras, radios and other electrical goods.

This was one port where I enjoyed using the local bus service which cost pennies, to travel round the island, and this I did on several occasions. On my first visit there, Cathy, one of the stewardesses and I shared a bus with several local ladies laden with baskets of fruit and vegetables from the market. We rattled along unsurfaced roads following the coast for several miles, returning to the town through the centre of the island. The trip cost us 1/6d (12½p) each. We still had some time to spare so we boarded another bus going in the opposite direction. We got chatting to a local man who gave us a running commentary on all the places we passed through. He invited us into his home to meet his family, but we didn't have time, as the bus was returning to Suva immediately and we had no idea when the next one would arrive.

On the way, we came to a fairly large village of straw huts where we found the women washing clothes in the river, pounding the clothes with stones. All were dressed in brightly-coloured kaftans and were laughing and joking among themselves.

We also enjoyed a bit of luxury when we visited Fiji, as it had several large hotels. The Tradewinds Hotel, set on a hill with a magnificent view of the bay and of our ship, was a favourite, as well as the Isa Lei Hotel with its isolated gardens, posh restaurant and large swimming pool. We liked to enjoy the good food and drink of these establishments and relax by the pool.

I could never have afforded these luxuries on my meagre salary, but the ship's surgeon Mike, as well as getting his salary from P&O, was able to charge passengers for any treatment received. He looked on this money as "extra" and spent it freely on his staff and close friends. I was lucky to be included in this select group and enjoyed his largesse on many occasions.

It was in the Tradewinds Hotel in Suva that I first tasted Mai Tai, a cocktail of rum, orange Curacao, lime juice and rock candy syrup. Mai Tai means "good" in Tahitian, so it's likely that the drink originated in the island of Tahiti. Our drinks were served in tall glasses adorned with flowers and fruit and tasted divine. They were also lethal. We had several under our belts before we realised the potency of the innocent-looking drink and we had to get a taxi back to the ship. Mai Tai became one of our favourite drinks, but in future we respected its strength and limited our consumption accordingly.

On another of our visits to Fiji, a bus was hired and a group led by the Staff Captain visited the Nausori Orphanage to hand over a donation, the proceeds of a crew concert held on board. The children in the orphanage were wholly of Indian origin, the Fijian culture being more family-orientated, with a good social network, thereby ensuring the children were well looked after if they were orphaned. I spent an enjoyable two hours playing with some of the children. I was "adopted" for the afternoon by a sad little girl of six (I thought she was about four) who had a hole in her heart but with no hope of treatment. There were 54 children in the home and only four adults. They had no electricity, no hot water and cooked on open fires. They had only recently had toilets installed.

At the time of our visit I read in the local newspaper that the number of Indians living in Fiji was rising and the population would soon be almost equal to that of the native Fijians. It was feared that the culture of Fiji could be permanently changed if the native Fijians didn't become actively involved in the running of the islands and in the saving of the Fijian way of life. The authorities were calling on the Fijian people to take note before it was too late.

Lautoka was another port in Fiji I enjoyed. A miniature railway plied between the town and the docks. It was normally used to ferry sugar-cane from the fields to the port, but when a cruise ship arrived, the train took over passenger-ferrying duties.

I was lucky enough to be given a free ticket for an afternoon bus trip to the other side of the island and the scenery there was equally spectacular. We passed many small islets covered in palm trees and with groups of occupied straw huts in the middle. At every turn we found lovely sandy coves edged with palm trees. In the centre of the island we bumped over dirt tracks between fields of sugar-cane and stopped at several small villages consisting of about a dozen or so thatched huts. We saw people ploughing the fields with two bullocks and a one-bladed, primitive–looking plough. Here again, we saw women washing their clothes in a stream at the side of the road.

As well as giving us a musical welcome to Fiji, we were usually serenaded by a Fijian choir when we left the Islands. The final song in their repertoire was always Isa Lei, Fiji's song of farewell which is sung to departing visitors. This haunting song, sung in Fijian, was so beautiful, that I always made sure if possible, to be on deck to hear it on our departure.

The weather wasn't always hot and sunny in the Pacific, and when we reached Pago Pago (pronounced Pango Pango) in American Samoa, we had to make a hasty exit twelve hours ahead of schedule as the islands were expecting a hurricane and the residents were busy tying down their straw huts with ropes and stones. We could have been marooned there for up to a week, as it was a tricky manoeuvre getting in and out of the harbour even in good weather. Soon after leaving Pago Pago we ran headlong into the hurricane. The wind howled, tearing the spray from the waves and sending it high into the air. Rain lashed down and the sea battered our little ship as she pitched and tossed valiantly through the – anything but! – Pacific Ocean.

Because of rough weather, *Iberia* was unable to enter Hilo Bay in Hawaii, so we carried on to Honolulu on the island of Oahu. Oahu was spectacular. The beaches were long and flat and edged with golden sand and elegant palm trees. The sea was a wonderful shade of blue and the sun shone non-stop every day we were there. The temperature in Hawaii is usually in the region of 75° the whole year round, and as the trade winds blow constantly, they keep everything cool and bearable. My first visit lasted three days and I set out to see as much of Honolulu and the island of Oahu as I could, in between my switchboard duties. On the first day a group of us caught a bus to Pearl Harbour where we boarded a naval launch to Ford Island on which stands the Arizona Memorial.

On 7th December 1941 the Japanese attacked Pearl Harbour, an act that led to the United States entering the Second World War. One thousand, one hundred and seventy-seven sailors were killed on the battleship *USS Arizona* that day, and the remains of the ship lie below the memorial built in their memory.

The *Arizona* was the first ship to be struck by the bombs and there were parts of her still visible. The guides at the memorial were all ex-servicemen who were survivors of the tragedy and their contribution brought home to us the horror of what had happened and the shocking effect it had had on them. It was a very moving experience for us.

Pearl Harbour was also the temporary resting place of the aircraft carrier *USS Enterprise*, which we could see tucked away round a corner. She was massive. When she was launched in 1960, the *Enterprise* was the first ever nuclear-powered aircraft carrier. She was fitted with eight nuclear reactors, was over 1,100 feet long and carried a crew of 4,600.

The *Enterprise* had recently been riven by a series of explosions, caused by a rocket on an F-4 Phantom jet overheating and blowing up. The resulting fire destroyed 15 aircraft and killed 27 sailors. Three hundred and fourteen sailors were seriously injured. The ship wasn't idle for long however, and was soon back at sea where she enjoyed a further 48 years of active service before being decommissioned in February 2017.

Next morning I walked about three miles to the dramatic natural setting of the National Memorial Cemetery of the Pacific. The "Punchbowl," as it is called, was formed about 75,000 to 100,000 years ago during a long period of volcanic activity. In 1943 the site was donated to the US War Department by the Governor of Hawaii for use as a national cemetery, and in 1969 it held the graves of over 13,000 American soldiers and sailors who died during WWII. From the top, there were wonderful views of Honolulu and the surrounding area, and the warm, gentle sunny weather made the trip very enjoyable.

In Honolulu however, the city was buzzing. The fast-moving traffic on the wide freeways was relentless and crossing the road was a nightmare. About a hundred yards away, through the palm-lined gardens bordering the main road, it was very different. Waikiki Beach was calm and completely sheltered from the noise and pollution of the busy road and I had a wonderful four hours there. I bought a hotdog and a coffee for my lunch and had a solitary picnic on the sand, watching the surfers and outrigger canoes riding the surf. I had a swim in the lukewarm water and enjoyed people-watching and just chilling out. The soft sound of Hawaiian guitar music occasionally wafted in my direction, completing an experience that was unforgettable. I walked back to the ship in time for sailing at five o'clock that afternoon.

An overnight stop in Noumea, capital of New Caledonia, was marred by the arrest of three bedroom stewards who were locked up for fighting in the street. One of the Radio Officers was sent to the Police Station to try to have them released, but he too was arrested and spent an uncomfortable night in the cells. They were released in time for sailing next day, but all four had been severely beaten by the police and were nursing black eyes and multiple bruises. There didn't appear to be any point in complaining to the authorities, so the ship slunk away, in silence, at sailing time.

I had a few hours off on my next visit to Auckland and took advantage of the crew tour which took us along the Hibiscus Coast to some hot springs. What I remember most about this part of New Zealand was how like England and the Borders of Scotland it looked. Tree-fringed green fields were dotted with fluffy, white sheep. It was a scene of peace and tranquillity and unfortunately brought on a severe dose of homesickness.

We were treated to a demonstration of Maori singing and dancing on board that evening. It was wonderful. I loved the slow, lilting, slightly twangy sound of the Maori voices and the song that sticks in my memory, and which was sung every time we left a New Zealand port, was "Now is the Hour." This was an early twentieth-century folk song which had Maori words added in 1915 and was sung as a farewell to New Zealand soldiers going to war. It always brought a tear to my eye.

On our return to Sydney, *Iberia* spent seven days in port when the ship was shut down completely for routine maintenance. We had no water, no light, no air-conditioning and no hot food. Luckily, we had no passengers either. I can't imagine this happening on a cruise ship nowadays. We still had to do our shifts on the switchboard, but during the daytime only, so by helping each other out, we were all able to get a fair bit of time off. With only cold food on offer on board ship, most nights a group of us went ashore to eat and this is where I met Ian, an electrician on *Oriana*, and with whom I became quite friendly. We enjoyed a few days sightseeing together in Sydney before *Oriana* sailed.

I took advantage of our week-long stay in Sydney to visit The Blue Mountains. This fantastic range of mountains west of the city is so named because from Sydney, they look blue. According to the Australian Tourist Board advertising literature, in the hot sun, the vast forests of eucalyptus trees discharge a fine mist of oil from their leaves. The mist refracts light, which makes the haze look blue from a distance.

My day-long trip also visited the Jenolan Caves, which nestled deep in a river valley. The winding access road to the caves was picturesque but hazardous. We seemed to be on the top of the mountain range for much of the way, looking down over the tops of mountains stretching for miles into the distance. There had been extensive fires in the Blue Mountains some weeks before my visit and all the trees for miles around were burnt black, with not a patch of undergrowth or a blade of grass to be seen.

To try to jolt my memory of my visit, I visited online, the official site of the Jenolan Caves. I found that now there are twelve caves open to the public with several tours a day to each cave. All I remember from my visit in 1969 was that we were the only bus tour there, we visited just one cave, and the visit lasted no time at all.

Our tour also passed through the town of Katoomba, home to Australia's most famous tourist site, The Three Sisters. Legend has it they were three beautiful women who had fallen in love with three men from a tribe in the foothills. The tribe prohibited any union between the sisters and their lovers, and a battle ensued. A witch doctor from the village turned the women to stone to prevent them from coming to any harm, but he was killed in the battle and no-one else knew how to undo his spell.

No visit to Sydney would be complete without a trip to the famous Bondi Beach. My colleague Rose and I packed a picnic and took a bus there. We sat on the golden sand and watched the huge rollers pounding on the shore. Surfers performed fantastic feats on their surf boards. The semi-circular beach is about three-quarters of a mile long, but its beauty was a little diminished by the sight of a great shark net suspended across the mouth of the bay.

Botany Bay was another place on my list and two friends and I took the local bus there. It poured rain all day and the stormy sea made me feel sorry for the prisoners who had landed there two hundred years ago when it was a penal colony. When the ship left Sydney three days later it was still raining. The area had had no rain for several weeks, so I didn't begrudge the Australians their downpour.

We arrived in Singapore at ten o'clock on the morning of 22nd February, and as I had finished my shift at nine o'clock that morning, a friend and I were already standing at the gangway ready to go ashore as soon as we docked. Change Alley, Singapore's famous shopping street, was our first stop.

The history of Change Alley dates back to 1819. According to Wikipedia, it started as a trading centre for mainly Chinese dealers who traded in pepper, copra and tin. In the 1930s it started to become a tourist attraction and by the 1950s it was selling clothes, watches, toys, crafts, souvenirs and tailoring and cobbler services.

By the time I visited Singapore, the alley consisted of small shops, makeshift tables, or even just boxes of goods lying on the floor, and from which the sellers produced their goods as soon as anyone looked interested. Roving sellers would pounce on the unsuspecting browser and, like magicians, produce watches, pens and other small goods from their clothing, hoping for a sale. The alley was open to the air, but there were parts that had awnings, plastic sheets, cardboard and other materials stretched above the stalls in an effort to keep out the rain, not always successfully.

Change Alley was narrow with hardly room for more than two or three persons to pass comfortably. It was a bit stuffy and very congested, but it had character and I loved the busy atmosphere. According to my diary, the streets around Change Alley were "very poor-looking with open drains, tatty buildings and washing lines all over the place." I loved watching people strike a bargain, which they did all the time. No-one paid the asking price for anything. The jewel colours of the bales of Thai silk on sale caught my eye and I managed to pluck up enough courage to conclude a bargain on a dress length of emerald green.

Afternoon tea at Raffles Hotel was also on our itinerary and I

The Three Sisters and Blue Mountains.

was suitably impressed. The main entrance hall/lounge was large and spacious and furnished with rattan furniture and cool-coloured furnishings. The waiters glided noiselessly between the tables serving tea in pretty china crockery on crisp white linen.

By the time I'd finished my second shift of the day, it was midnight and all my friends had gone ashore. It looked as though I would have to spend the evening on board. Rescue came from an unusual source. Pete, the chief baker, was a man in his fifties who'd been to sea for nigh on thirty years and could understand my disappointment at missing the opportunity to see Singapore by night. He offered to take me ashore.

We took a taxi into Chinatown, to a restaurant in a small side street well away from the tourist spots. Pete was greeted like a long-lost friend and he told me this was one of his regular haunts while in the city. There was not another European face to be seen. It was here that I tasted the most wonderful Chinese food ever.

We started off with shark's fin soup, now frowned upon, but I didn't think about these things in the sixties. It was delicious. Several piping hot dishes were brought to the table and, although I can't remember exactly what we ate, I do know that it all tasted superb. The waiters appeared to know Pete quite well and they danced attendance on us. By the way the waiters chuckled and appeared to tease Pete, I think he may have given them the impression that he'd managed to "pull a young bird" but I was enjoying my dinner so much that I didn't contradict them.

I'd heard all about Bugis (pronounced Boogy) Street, in Singapore, the street where the trans-women, or "lady-boys" congregated nightly, making the street Singapore's top tourist destination. Pete was reluctant to take me there saying it was not the place for young ladies! I would have to wait for my visit to Bugis Street. We went instead to the cinema where I saw a film featuring Edinburgh City Police Pipe Band led by my old friend and colleague Pipe Major Ian MacLeod, bringing on another bout of the dreaded homesickness. A trishaw ride back to the ship through the mean streets of Singapore raised my spirits.

Next morning I had a chat with one of the waiters from the ship, a nineteen-year-old lad who was on his first trip to sea. He told me he had been chatting up one of the "girls" in Bugis Street and she invited him back to her flat. Thinking he was on to something good, he agreed and as things "hotted up" in the bedroom he suddenly realised that his "girl" was in fact a man. He grabbed his clothes and ran. He had no idea where he was. The flat was in one of the rougher parts of the city, but luckily it was in the harbour area and he ran in the right direction, not stopping until he was safely in his cabin. It was an experience he wasn't likely to forget in a hurry.

I was looking forward to our four days in Hong Kong. As *Iberia* sailed towards Ocean Terminal at around 4 pm, we could see very little of the colony as it was shrouded in mist. This was Hong Kong's winter and it was very cold. While the ship was being manoeuvred slowly towards its berth, a junk drew alongside, a rope ladder was thrown up, and what happened next was like something out of a film. Dozens of Chinamen poured out of the junk, up the rope ladder which had been secured to the ship's rail by one of the crew, and over the side of the ship. They looked like a line of ants. These were the famous Hong Kong tailors coming in for an early kill. It was said by officers and crew that if you stood still for just a few seconds, it was all that was required for the tailor

Hong Kong harbour.

to measure you for a suit.

Next day I booked a tour of Hong Kong Harbour. Our motorised junk chugged through the Yau Ma Tei Typhoon Shelter, home to about 150,000 "Boat People" who lived on their boats and rarely set foot on land, and Aberdeen Harbour, home of several floating restaurants. It was bitterly cold and I was chilled to the marrow, but I enjoyed the experience.

February the 28th was my 28th birthday and I was taken out to lunch by Mike, the ship's surgeon. We crossed Victoria Harbour on the famous Star Ferry to the Mandarin Hotel. As we stepped into the lobby of the hotel, it took our breath away. Vast walls of marble and bronze rose on two sides. An enormous chandelier glittered from the high ceiling and wide carpeted stairs rose to several lounges above. As we sat in the bar having pre-lunch drinks, we heard a familiar voice. We had a guessing game, and we both won: it was Jimmy Edwards, the famous comedy actor.

Our lunch was in the 25th floor restaurant with magnificent views of the harbour and beyond. We had a wonderful seven-course feast, but I can only recall one of the courses: crabmeat shaped like a chicken leg and eaten with the fingers.

It was back on the ferry to Kowloon for an afternoon of shopping. We roamed through narrow streets of tiny shops jammed together and packed with goods from all over the world, but mainly from China. Aromatic stalls piled high with colourful spices, odd fruits and vegetables, sat cheek-by-jowl with kitchen paraphernalia and various electrical goods.

Crew salaries were paid at the end of each voyage but we could draw on this at the main ports of call. I collected a "sub" in Hong Kong and had my present-buying spree in the larger duty-free shops.

When we arrived in any port, the first thing I did was familiarise myself with the emergency information and local telephone numbers and this was to stand me in good stead when I was on duty that night and we had a fire in one of the baggage rooms. A steward rang me with details and I immediately contacted the local fire brigade, then I called the officer of the watch on duty on the bridge. The fire brigade responded quickly and the fire was extinguished with not too much damage. I later got a thank-you from the Captain for my quick thinking.

The passengers on this particular trip were not great spenders, and came back to the ship for every meal. Very few ventured ashore in the evening. Every night, from nine o'clock onwards, the telephone exchange was inundated with orders for tea and toast. The passengers even asked for a film to be shown every night we were in Hong Kong.

It didn't cost that much to enjoy Hong Kong. There was a wonderful hustle and bustle about the place, of movement, noise and smells, especially in the evening when hundreds of food stalls were set up in the streets. There was street theatre and jocular hustling by vendors trying to sell their wares, so that just strolling about was a joy. It all felt very safe and my friends and I took every opportunity to experience the street life of Hong Kong after dark. We enjoyed sampling the Hong Kong street food and came to no harm whatsoever.

Hong Kong was a wonderful sight at night even when shrouded in mist. The mist was low and the neon signs on the tall buildings that covered every hill, looked as if they were rising out of the clouds. Two American naval ships and one British ship were anchored in the bay, dressed overall. The American ships sported one string of lights like something in a funfair, whereas the British ship was illuminated from head to foot. There was no comparison in the beauty stakes.

Iberia sailed from Hong Kong at ten o'clock in the evening of 1st March and we had yet another incident to add to our chequered history. I was on deck to watch us sail. We were just getting up speed when there was a loud crash and cries from the sea. Iberia had hit a junk which cut across the ship's bows. The junk was cut clean in two and we could see bodies floundering in the water. The ship was unable to stop and it was left to the harbour authorities to save the struggling family. We heard later that they had all been rescued.

We spent a day sailing through the China Sea before arriving at Manila in the Philippines. We had been advised not to go ashore alone, and even when in company, to remain alert at all times. Manila was known to be a dangerous city. The year before, my brother Alistair, who was in the Royal Navy, went ashore in Manila with a friend. They were walking along one of the main streets and happened to look down an alleyway running at right angles. There they saw an American sailor being set-upon and stabbed by a group of Philippino men. Alistair and his friend got the fright of their lives.

Sailing through the Philippines parallel to the shore was a treat. We moved slowly and were able to see at close hand the towns and villages we passed by. Our route took us through the Sulu Sea past the town of Zamboanga and into the Celebes Sea and then the Banda Sea. We sailed through many small islands where the water was calm and smooth as glass and there were flying fish in abundance. It was here that we recorded a temperature of 115° F on the bridge.

Our next port was Darwin on the north coast of Australia. This was in 1969 before the town was devastated by Cyclone Tracy on Christmas Eve 1974. It was extremely hot that day: 102° F and very humid. Norma and I took a taxi into the town centre, one long street resembling a scene from a Spaghetti Western. There wasn't a soul to be seen; the shops were closed and the few people on the streets were from the ship. Norma and I cooled down with a cold beer in a pretty rough bar before heading back to the ship.

Sailing eastwards along the north coast of Australia, the ship travelled close to the land but nowhere could we see any sign of habitation, just mile after mile of scrubland. We had a spell when the weather turned cold. For several days the surgery was overflowing every morning and afternoon and there were extra calls for the doctor out-with surgery hours. In a letter to my mother I wrote, "The Dispenser is kept busy dishing out codeine and Gee's Linctus, which is what everyone gets irrespective of their illness." We did however, have an emergency when a woman had to have her appendix removed by the ship's surgeon.

It was around this time that I was asked if I wanted to buy a bottle of Chivas Regal whisky at a ridiculously low price. When we arrived in Sydney a few weeks previously, at the end of our outward voyage from Southampton, nearly £2,000 worth of spirits and cigarettes had disappeared from one of the holds. The Police were called and a thorough search of the ship was undertaken. A quantity of spirits was found stashed away, presumably by some of the crew, but a large amount was never found. Now, some weeks later, I was offered a bottle of what was obviously stolen whisky. There was still a remnant of the policewoman about me, and I didn't fancy being charged with reset if it all came to light, so I declined the offer.

Niuafo'ou is a small, doughnut-shaped, volcanic island, the most northerly of the Tongan archipelago, situated in the southern Pacific Ocean, between Fiji and Samoa. It is better known as Tin Can Island because of its unusual method of sending and receiving mail. In 1882 a plantation manager, William Travers, found himself marooned on the island. As the only white man there, he wanted to communicate with the outside world, and tried to devise a way of doing so. About a couple of miles off-shore, he could see ships passing, but with no harbour and no beaches, and the island consisting of steep cliffs, it was impossible to anchor or even land a rowing boat.

Travers wrote a letter to the Tongan postal authorities, asking them to seal his mail in a ship's biscuit tin, and arrange for the captain of one of the Union Steamship vessels to throw it overboard as they passed the island. The arrangement was that the

Tin can mail delivery.

captain would sound his siren and a swimmer from the island would collect the tin. Travers wrapped his letter in grease-proof paper and tied it to a stick. He then asked the strongest swimmer on the island to swim out to the next ship that passed and hand the letter over to the captain. So began the Tin Can Mail Service.

Sometime during the reign of Queen Salote, which was from 1918 to 1965, one of the "postmen" was killed by a shark and the Queen ordered that in future, the mail would be collected by out-rigger canoe. By 1969, the sea around Tin Can Island was a regular stop for cruise ships, although passengers were unable to land there because of a lack of suitable landing places. The islanders had obviously got their act together and organised a postal service, still using the outrigger canoes. On board ship, we bought our postcards and stamps and they were dropped off in the "biscuit tin" to be collected by the islanders. The cards were then franked with the Tin Can Island official logo and were picked up by the next cruise ship to call at the island. It could take many months for the cards to reach their destination and I arrived home in Rosemarkie long before my postcard did.

A heavy sea was running when we neared Niuafo'ou, but in the distance we could see a tiny outrigger canoe manned by four men, battling against the huge waves. The waves were so high that sometimes the canoe disappeared for several seconds, but soon came bobbing up again. When they got close enough to ensure a successful recovery, the tin cans of mail were tossed into the sea. Apparently not just mail was thrown from the ship that day. A few little luxuries were added by the staff in the galley, but unfortunately my notes don't say what these luxuries were. The weather was dull, misty and wet, and as we sailed along the coast of the island, as close inshore as we could safely go, I could see high cliffs, where the waves, lashing against the rocks, spouted spectacular fountains of foam into the air.

The Tongan archipelago is a Polynesian Kingdom comprising over 170 islands, many of which are uninhabited. The main island of Tongatapu was everything a south sea island should be: it had blue skies, beautiful beaches and wall-to-wall sunshine. The approach to Nuku Alofa, capital of Tongatapu, was through miles of coral reefs, rather tricky for the ship's navigator, but wonderful for the passengers and crew who lined the decks watching the many shoals of multi-coloured fish that swam around us in a sea that was verging on turquoise. Several statuesque Tongan men could be seen standing waist deep on the reef, spear fishing. They appeared to be standing on one leg, but looked perfectly comfortable. All the time I watched the fishermen, I didn't see any of them catch anything, so maybe they were there for the delectation of the ship's passengers rather than for catching their supper.

With my friend Henni, I took a taxi/bicycle from the ship to the straw market where we watched Tongan dancers swaying in their grass skirts to the beautiful music of a male voice choir accompanied by a group of several twangy guitars. The straw market was overflowing with expertly crafted wares and it was easy to be seduced by the cheap prices and the persuasive stallholders. I bought a basket and a sun hat and when I got back to the ship I left them in my cabin. When I returned in the evening, the cabin was over-run with ants. I had to have the cabin sprayed to get rid of the infestation. The bo'sun was busy for a few days fumigating the passenger cabins, as they too had had a buying spree in the straw market.

The calm and peace of Tongatapu was shattered during the afternoon when we had a terrible accident on board. A Goanese crew member, who was painting the side of the ship, fell on to the quay and into the water. It was three-quarters of an hour before his body was recovered. The ship was delayed overnight as the Ship's Surgeon had to perform a post mortem on the man and he and the Chief Officer had to visit the British Consulate where there was an enquiry into the accident. The passengers subsequently organised a collection and £150 was given to his dependents.

We had five days in Sydney in preparation for our six week voyage home via the Cape of Good Hope. As soon as the ship berthed at Circular Quay, I joined a bus tour to the Hawkesbury River. This consisted of a two-hour launch trip up the river, then a stop for lunch and return to Sydney by bus. We stopped at a koala bear sanctuary where I found these cuddly nocturnal animals snoozing in the trees. Occasionally one would open an eye to look at these strange people "ooohing" and "aaahing" and taking loads of photos. Several kangaroos strolled around the grounds, some with their joeys peeping out of the pouch.

It was during this stop-over in Sydney that I had the first of several visitors to the ship. Those were the days when all you needed to get someone on board was permission from the Purser. Nowadays, security is so tight, the public can't even get within a hundred yards of the ship, and permission to get on board has to be obtained from company headquarters in London. I'm told it is rarely granted.

Kay Summerfield, an Australian who lived in Brisbane but who had met and married an Inverness man when she toured Europe some years before, came to the ship with her mother and her three sons. I had a lovely day with them. They had a tour of the ship, then lunch on board, and in the afternoon we all went on a boat trip round Sydney Harbour.

Sunday was wet but it didn't deter me and I went ashore alone for a walk round the city. As I was passing Sydney Town Hall, having lost my way trying to get back to Circular Quay, I saw that the English Chamber Orchestra conducted by Daniel Barenboim and featuring Jacqueline Du Pre, was playing there, beginning in two hours' time. With the prospect of another quiet night on board, which I didn't relish, I went straight in and bought a ticket, then sat down to fish and chips in a nearby café. I emerged from the concert into a downpour, but the music had lifted my spirits so much that I treated myself to a taxi. It was well worth it. I was broke but happy. Next day we sailed for home.

When there were several days at sea, the crew made their own entertainment in the form of "pour-outs" (ship-speak for drinks parties) and dinners, usually in private cabins or on the private decks. Specially printed invitations were sent out, courtesy of a friendly ship's printer and it was just as well, as there were so many parties, it was easy to miss one. Surgeon Mike held regular curry nights on the hospital deck. One in particular I remember, was while we were travelling westwards through the Indian Ocean and had eight days at sea. The Goanese stewards were fantastic cooks and Mike's man was exceptional. We had three courses, salmon, chicken and lamb. The night was soft and balmy and we downed a few bottles of rich red wine. We usually had a singsong afterwards and a few games. On this occasion David, the Assistant Surgeon, got a bit over-enthusiastic, and for his party piece did a Zulu Dance followed by a striptease, right down to where he twirled his y-fronts on his little finger and tossed them overboard. No-one could beat that.

There was plenty to occupy the crew on these long days at sea. I was a member of the Rosettes, the ladies' darts team led by Rose, my colleague in the telephone exchange. The team consisted of telephonists and stewardesses and we took our place on the team when we were available. We also had a barbecue on board for the officers and crew and it ended with a brilliant sing-song, led by Gordon, Radio Operator and Rory, Deck Officer.

There was also a great deal of talent among the Goanese and European crew and this was put to good use when a concert was held in the crew rec room. The audience was made up of crew members and officers and was well attended. An activity such as this helped keep morale at a high level during the long days at sea.

During our journey across the Indian Ocean, three stowaways were found in the hold. Two of them consisted of an Irishman and his three-year old son. The man's wife had left him and he wanted

Pour out on hospital deck, Iberia.

to go home; the other was a Brit who wanted to get back to the UK but couldn't afford the fare. Stowaways were usually disembarked at the next port of call, but South Africa refused to accept them so they had their wish and all made it to the UK courtesy of P&O.

I also renewed the acquaintance of an albatross and I woke one morning at four-thirty and went on deck to watch an amazing electric storm. Great flashes of lightning lit up the sky as far as the eye could see. When we arrived in Cape Town I saw the most wonderful sunset, the best I've ever seen. The sky turned orange and several shades of red as the sun descended slowly below the horizon.

There was never a dull moment on board and sometimes things got a bit out of hand. One of the nightwatchmen, who thought he was the same rank as the Captain, was rather lazy. I asked him to carry out a task for the Purser, but as the request hadn't come directly from the Purser, he refused. When I threatened to report him, he became abusive and began dashing about telling everyone he was being blamed for my failure to pass on the message. He didn't get away with it however, and was given a good telling off next morning by the Chief Steward.

A few days later, Norma had a hilarious incident involving the same man. He wasn't very popular on board and he'd fallen out with one of the bedroom stewards who chased him through the ship and into the telephone exchange. Norma, all of five-foot-nothing and seven stones, tried to calm down the bedroom steward while the nightwatchman hid behind the switchboard and refused to budge. When he did eventually emerge, it was to lock himself in the Purser's office where he stayed for several hours, peering through the window at the activities outside. Even the intervention of two officers couldn't persuade him to come out, and it was several hours later, when he was sure that his would-be attacker had abandoned the pursuit, that he calmed down and went back to his cabin.

I'm surprised there were not many more incidents of this nature as the accommodation for the crew left a lot to be desired. The galley staff lived in what was called the "bear pit," down in the bowels of the ship, eight or ten to a cabin.

"The Channels" is a condition that affects all seafarers when they are nearing the English Channel and are excited about getting home and seeing their loved ones. I got it big time! During our crossing of the Bay of Biscay and on our journey up the English Channel, I was in a state of high excitement. I talked too much, I couldn't sleep and I couldn't concentrate to read.

We slid into our berth at Tilbury docks at eight o'clock on the morning of 22nd May. After the passengers had disembarked, the ship moved out midstream where we dropped anchor until 5pm. I was desperate to catch my flight to Inverness, so as soon as we docked I was first down the gangway. I took a taxi to the West London Air Terminal which was located on Cromwell Road, Kensington, far from the airport. When I got there I found I'd missed the bus for the flight. I booked into a hotel. In the restaurant I met a young Australian teacher who had also missed his flight and was having to spend a night in London. We had our meal together and he offered to take me out on the town, but I was so tired and so disappointed at missing my flight that I turned him down. Next morning I was up at 5.30am and caught the 7.45am flight to Inverness via Aberdeen.

Part 2

Mediterranean Cruising

June 1969 to September 1969

On 11th June 1969 I arrived at Tilbury Docks to re-join Iberia, and met up with my new cabin mate Elsie, a lady in her fifties who had been at sea for seventeen years. Iberia was now embarking on a series of Mediterranean cruises.

I got on extremely well with Elsie. She was interesting to talk to and full of fun. Every night after dinner she disappeared down to the galley, returning to the cabin with two Irish Coffees. She was very fond of her Irish coffee and eventually I had to make excuses to be elsewhere, as I realised that I was an amateur in the drinking stakes compared to Elsie.

Many of the Mediterranean ports were still small and undeveloped in the late sixties. Very few had facilities for a large ship to tie up alongside, so disembarkation was usually by ship's tender. At most of these ports there was little laid on for those of us who didn't go on the organised tours. A few stalls selling local crafts and souvenirs were set up on the quay, but in the towns the locals just got on with their lives and everything closed for siesta in the afternoon.

I had visited Ceuta in 1967 when I was a passenger on the SS *Chusan*, so I was looking forward to another visit. Ceuta is one of two populated Spanish territories on mainland Africa. It is about seven square miles in size and sits on the north coast of Africa, sharing a western border with Morocco. According to Wikipedia, Ceuta was part of Cadiz Province until it became an autonomous city of Spain in 1995 when the city's Statute of Autonomy was enacted. In a situation similar to the territorial claims of Spain over Gibraltar, Morocco has repeatedly called for Spain to transfer the sovereignty of Ceuta to Morocco, but without success. To date this is an ongoing problem.

It is interesting to read modern tourist information about the Mediterranean ports. According to Wikipedia, Ceuta is now a bustling city of over 85,000 people. In 1992 a five-miles-long fence was built around the enclave, supposedly to stop illegal immigration and smuggling.

In 1967 when I visited Ceuta as a passenger on board *Chusan*, there was no such barrier. When my friends and I went ashore, the town was deserted. We happened to meet up with the ship's musicians who were heading to the beach for a picnic so we decided to join them. We obviously took a wrong turning somewhere, because we ended up at a border crossing into Morocco. My friends and I were a bit worried about crossing into another country, but our musician companions had no such qualms. They assured the border guards that we were simply going to swim and have a picnic, so after surrendering our passports, we were allowed to cross into one of Morocco's wonderful sandy beaches. I didn't really enjoy myself however, as the thought of my passport lying in a border shed just along the coast preyed on my mind and I was glad when it was time to get back to the ship.

On this occasion I went ashore with Norma and we were disappointed to find that, following the Spanish custom, everything closed for siesta in the afternoon. We lost our way at one point and ended up in a rough area, but managed to find a café that was open for business and sat there for an hour chatting to the waiters who were keen to practise their English. Ceuta was a duty-free port, so when the shops opened at about four o'clock, there was just enough time to stock up on a few bottles of wine and head back to the ship for sailing at six.

Alghero, capital of Sardinia, stands on the north-west coast of the island. Encircled by the old city walls, the centre of the town has narrow cobbled streets and squares. It was an absolute gem of a place, full of atmosphere. Alghero also boasted a wonderful cathedral: the Cathedral of Santa Maria, but curiously, it was closed when we visited. We had to be content to wander the streets, sit at an open-air cafe and relax.

Cannes was expensive. I wrote to my mother saying that two cups of coffee cost 7/6, a fortune in 1969 but only 36 pence today. On the bus taking us into town I took note of a conversation I over-heard between two elderly female passengers. "I'm not spending any money in France or Spain," declared one. "I'm saving my money for Gibraltar. I'm not giving my money to our enemies." As three of the ports visited by the ship were Spanish and one was French, she wouldn't be spending much on that particular cruise. I too, didn't spend much in Cannes. It was a hot day and I went ashore in the morning with Henni. We strolled along the main boulevard past the magnificent hotels, hoping we'd bump into someone famous, which we didn't, then we walked through the market. Most of the beaches were private, being owned by the hotels, but we found a spot where we sat for a couple of hours and soaked up the sun.

In 1969, Palma, Majorca was a refined, small town with a distinct Spanish feel. Together with three female friends I went ashore for a meal. We preferred to avoid the tourist areas, and on this occa-sion we found a small back-street pub where we drank cube-libre (Bacardi and coke) and ate odd-looking, but quite delicious Tapas, followed by fresh seafood, caught that morning, we were told. The bar was crowded with local fishermen and we became the centre of attention for a couple of hours as the men practised their limited English and told us tales of their dangerous life on small boats in all kinds of weather. No regular hours for them: they lowered their nets when the fish arrived no matter what time of day or night.

On a later visit to Palma, I fell in with a couple of cadets from the Bureau and the Assistant Shore Excursions Officer who suggested we go on a tour of the Caves of Drach. The caves were located on the east coast of Majorca near the town of Porto Cristo. We walked for some distance into the main cave before coming upon a vast lake, Lake Martel, and took our seats for a classical concert by a small group of musicians. It was quite dark in the cave with a few lights strategically placed for the maximum effect. Then the lights went out, the music started and three brightly lit boats, one of which contained the musicians, appeared as if from nowhere, to glide across the lake towards us. The orchestra played for about twenty minutes, before wending its way further into the cave. Our small group of visitors then boarded the two remaining boats and were rowed across the lake where we disembarked. It was a wonderful experience which I enjoyed very much.

Next on our tour was a visit to a factory which made the famous "Majorica" pearls. I had been told that Hong Kong was the place to buy cultured pearls and I intended to buy some on my next visit, so I wasn't tempted to buy the man-made version, no matter how good they looked. I noticed from my diary that we also visited a wood carving factory, but I must have been short of cash at the time, because I didn't buy anything there either.

When we reached Gibraltar for an overnight stay, I went ashore with Elsie for a meal at a very grand hotel. In the bar later, we got chatting to two young men and Elsie was all for having a night on the town with them. I had a job getting her back to the ship.

Next day I caught the cable car to the top of the Rock to view the Barbary Macaques, Gibraltar's most famous residents. These tailless monkeys were very cute, but we were advised not to get too close as they tended to be vicious and could inflict a serious injury. They were also adept at stealing any food and belongings if they were not securely tied down or hidden away in pockets. A popular belief is that as long as the monkeys exist on Gibraltar, the territory will remain under British rule. Britain has long been involved in Gibraltar. According to the "History of Parliament" website, in 1704, during the War of the Spanish Succession, Admiral George Rooke, leading an Anglo-Dutch force, helped to capture Gibraltar when he took possession in the name of Queen Anne. This was legalised in 1713 when the Treaty of Utrecht ceded Gibraltar to the British Crown in perpetuity.

According to the "gibraltarmonkey" website, from 1915 to 1991 the monkey population was under the control of the British Army and an officer was appointed to supervise their welfare. The army budget included a food allowance of fruit, vegetables and nuts for the resident population. Three times the population dwindled to a dangerously low number, and each time the group was supplemented by monkeys imported from North Africa. During WWII the number was reduced to just seven, and on a visit to the Rock in 1944, Prime Minister Winston Churchill ordered that the numbers be replenished immediately. This was done by importing monkeys from Morocco and Algeria.

Following withdrawal of the British Garrison in 1991, the Government of Gibraltar assumed responsibility for the monkeys. Today they are managed by the Gibraltar Ornithological and Natural History Society. The monkeys number between 230 and 240, and live in six packs of between 25 and seventy each.

Vigo, in the north of Spain, was a lovely old Spanish town with narrow cobbled streets, steep hills and red-roofed houses. We had only a few hours in this port and it was very cold and wet, so I was quite happy to wander through the shops. Vigo had a reputation as the place to buy leather so I invested in a wonderful pair of soft brown leather boots which lasted me for many years.

We had a calm passage through the Bay of Biscay, which I describe in my diary as "like a millpond," and a few days later we disembarked our passengers in Southampton. We had a couple of days before the next cruise began. It is amazing what a difference two days can make, because when we entered the Bay of Biscay on our way south, it was extremely rough and many of the passengers were seasick. We encountered thick fog during the night and the ship's foghorn kept me awake for some time.

Funchal in Madeira was our first stop on this cruise and we were staying there overnight. In 1969 it was small and quiet with very little traffic on the roads. The streets of the town centre were cobbled and the buildings old and dust-coloured. The main street was wide and lined with the famous blue Jacaranda trees which, when in full bloom, were a wonderful sight. Madeira also had orchids galore, growing wild.

I never liked to miss a minute of the time available to go ashore and I was usually off the ship as soon as possible. I would then return to the ship to complete my shift on the switchboard and slip ashore again as soon as I finished work. I became adept at fitting in short visits to nearby sights and timing these to perfection.

On day two, I visited Funchal's indoor fish market. At six o'clock in the morning it was busy with buyers from the local hotels trying to drive a bargain with the many individual sellers. They appeared to go from stall to stall until they found what they were looking for at their preferred price. The housewives were also out in force driving a hard bargain.

Later, a friend and I got the bus to Monte, a small village up in the mountains. We found a restaurant with a viewpoint commanding a fantastic view of the whole of the town of Funchal spread out below. After lunch we walked back to the town through cobbled lanes and wonderful gardens and stumbled upon a winery. The gates were open and the place was deserted except for two elderly men who were climbing a ladder to the top of the great vats of wine and taking samples. They invited us to taste some of the wine.

No such thing as Health and Safety here, as we climbed the rickety ladder to the top of the vat and dipped in the stemless (broken) glasses the men were using for the testing, to sample the wine. It was delicious and we were told the wine was made in 1845. I'm not sure I believed them, but it was a soft, smooth wine and we had a second and third sample before we formed an opinion of its age. The men then gave us a conducted tour of the winery concluding at the official tasting area which was laid out with many dozens of small barrels of wine, but empty of visitors. We tasted quite a few before making our way, tipsily, back to the ship.

Ibiza was our next port of call. The island was unspoilt in 1969 with only one newly-built hotel a few miles out of the town. The narrow streets of the old fortified town which, we were told, was two thousand years old, climbed steeply upwards past old, pale stone buildings to the top of the hill, where Ibiza Cathedral stood in all its glory like a crown.

A taxi ride into the centre of the island took some friends and me past huge salt pans, salt being the main industry in Ibiza at this time. Driving through some small villages dotted about the island, we could see no tourist activity. Our taxi driver took us to a secluded beach which we had to ourselves for the rest of the day. We swam and frolicked on the sand and ate wonderful seafood paella in a conveniently placed taverna, which had no other customers all afternoon.

Barcelona was hot and sticky when we arrived so I waited until late afternoon before venturing ashore. Elsie and I strolled along the Ramblas, sampled tapas and drank ice cold beer while watching some flamenco dancers. I was on duty at midnight and as we were sailing at five o'clock that morning, I was kept busy all night, as were the night shift stewards, with orders for strong coffee, Horlicks or tea and toast, from the returning passengers, many the worse for wear after a night on the town. The Master at Arms was also kept busy as half the crew had gone ashore and returned drunk. It was an eventful evening and I was glad to get my head down at the end of my shift at six o'clock.

The Battle of Corunna took place on 16th January 1809 during the Peninsular War between the Spanish and the British under the command of Lieutenant General Sir John Moore on one side, and the French army of Napoleon on the other. Sir John Moore was injured in the battle and died on the battlefield, where he was hurriedly buried by his fellow officers. His death was later commemorated in the poem by Charles Wolfe, "The Burial of Sir John Moore in Corunna" and the words of the poem were engraved on a stone slab beside his grave.

I managed to get on a tour to the tomb of Sir John Moore. The Spanish guide insisted on reading the poem by Charles Wolfe in his Spanish accent which rather spoilt it. My mother loved poetry and had passed this love on to me, so I knew the poem quite well and didn't appreciate the Spanish Guide's recitation. I stayed behind when the group moved away and enjoyed it in solitary silence.

I looked on the internet for a modern photo of Sir John's tomb, and after 50 years the area is very different from what I remember. In 1969 the tomb was on a bare piece of land well away from the town of Corunna and near the sea. Today it appears to be in the midst of a built-up area, which may make it not quite as moving and atmospheric as I found it in 1969.

The Tower of Hercules, a lighthouse built in the first century and a prominent landmark at the entrance to Corunna Harbour was our next stop. My notes regarding the visit to the lighthouse are sparse and this may be because I noted in my diary that it was a wet, blustery day and I was feeling the cold.

The next Mediterranean cruise took us first to Lisbon where I booked a tour to Setubal. The bus travelled via the Pont 25 de Abril, a vast suspension bridge of two kilometres in length which was opened in 1966. The bridge connects Lisbon with the Almada region. On a hill at the southern end of the bridge stands a huge statue, the National Sanctuary of Christ the King which commands a superb view of Lisbon and the surrounding area.

Setubal was a lovely little village with beautiful scenery overlooking high cliffs and the sea below, but with not much else for the tourist. We wandered round the village square, had a coffee and got back on the bus for the journey back to Lisbon.

We had three days sailing through the Mediterranean on our way to Athens and this was when the staff parties were held to keep boredom at bay. I attended a curry party in the Dispenser's cabin and I'm not sure if it was the strong champagne cocktails or a dodgy curry, but we all felt fragile the next day and several of us had to forego the following two days of partying.

On our two-day visit to Piraeus, the port for the city of Athens, I was able to pack in several sights in my short time available. A bus tour of Athens took me to several fantastic archaeological sites, including the Acropolis. I ticked them off on my trusty copy of the Port Notes, with reminders to visit in more depth on another occasion. I left the tour at noon in the city centre and made a quick visit to the National Archaeological Museum where I wanted to view Zeus hurling a thunderbolt (or Poseidon throwing the trident!) It was a quick visit because the museum closed at one o'clock. After a picnic lunch in the National Gardens, a lovely park in the centre of Athens, I wandered through the city at my leisure. A tram transported me back to Piraeus in time for my evening shift.

Next day I went to the beach with David, the ship's junior doctor. We fell in with a group of engineers who were also heading that way and we all spent a wonderful morning swimming in the warm Mediterranean and soaking up the sun, eating from the beach stalls and in the case of the men, drinking too much. I had to be back on board for an afternoon shift so I didn't dare indulge, especially as I left the boys on the beach and had to find my own way back to the ship. In the evening a group of us took the bus into Athens where we viewed the amazing sight of an illuminated Acropolis and watched a Son et Lumiere in one of the parks.

On 21st July 1969, *Iberia* was cruising slowly past Stromboli, the active volcano off the coast of Sicily. I was off duty at the time and I sat on deck watching the smoke and fiery rocks spout from the cone and land in a plume of steam in the soft blue Mediterranean. At the same time, the ship was broadcasting over the loudspeakers, the first ever landing on the moon by American astronauts Armstrong and Aldrin.

Ajaccio, Corsica was our next stop and I had to work until 1pm. As we sailed at 4, all I had time for was a quick trip ashore to visit Napoleon's birthplace. It was closed!

While travelling home through the Bay of Biscay, we rendez-voused with an oil tanker to take on board two injured seamen who needed urgent medical attention. The injured men were placed on stretchers which were loaded on to a lifeboat. The lifeboat was lowered from the tanker and began its perilous journey towards Iberia. A rough sea and heavy fog didn't make it an easy transfer. As the two ships moved slowly in parallel through the water, keeping as safe a distance as possible between them, I watched anxiously from the deck. The lifeboat dipped into deep troughs then appeared to balance precariously on top of the huge waves. On reaching Iberia, the stretchers were carefully hoisted aboard through the lower gun-port door where many willing hands were available to rush them to safety. The men were badly burned and they were in the expert care of the medical department for the rest of the journey back to Southampton.

After five days spent in Bristol with my friend Gill, I arrived back on board *Iberia* to discover that Elsie had left and was replaced by Janet, a quietly spoken, refined lady of my own age. With another batch of cruisers aboard we headed down the Solent hoping Biscay was calm. It made such a difference to the mood of the passengers if the weather was good: they were pleasant, polite and ready for a chat. If the weather was bad they became rude, demanding and restless.

Quite often we would meet other ships of the line and an acknowledgement of their presence was always noted with a sounding of the ship's siren. On this occasion we sailed for a few miles down the Solent in line with *Chusan* and the Cunard liner, *RMS Carmania*, until we left *Carmania* behind and *Chusan* eventually sped off into the distance.

Monastir, Tunisia was an interesting stop. The people on the streets were Arabs dressed in long white robes and the few women that we saw, were in traditional black burqas with only their eyes visible. There were camels galore and plenty smells, some pungent and some pleasant. It was a small town with quite a few modern buildings, one supermarket and a row of about six small shops. All the other buildings were mosques, garages, offices and hotels.

Norma and I took a picnic to the beach and I couldn't resist the allure of the turquoise water. I was swimming along slowly when I felt a hand on my bottom. I looked round and a young boy was smiling at me and making comments which I didn't understand, but also making gestures which I did! I used a phrase I'd only just learned: Piss Off! He understood and vanished.

Palermo, capital of Sicily was a noisy city and you crossed the road at your peril. I went ashore in the afternoon with a friend and we were sitting on a wall outside the Post Office waiting for it to open when I was accosted by an old woman who objected to the length of my dress. The mini-skirt was in fashion at the time and my dress was pretty short. The woman caused quite a stir in the street as she tugged at the hem of my dress and shouted at me. Eventually one or two passers-by intervened and we managed to escape. We didn't get far however, when we realised that we were being followed by a policeman on a scooter, who sidled up to us making kissing noises and uttering suggestive remarks (I think). We hurried into the nearest café to get rid of him.

I didn't do what Ruth, a policewoman colleague of mine in Edinburgh did when she was accosted in Italy by a policeman on a scooter. She was a burly woman with many years' police service under her belt, and when the policeman sidled up to her and pinched her ample bottom, she lifted her fist and smacked him on the face, knocking him off his scooter. He called for assistance and a furious Ruth was arrested and taken to the local nick. When she started to give her side of the story to the reporting officer however, he appeared to find it funny and started to laugh. Eventually the whole station office was in an uproar. Ruth was sent on her way with a ticking-off, while the Italian policeman was left nursing his sore face and his injured pride.

You would think that having spent seven-and-a-half years as a policewoman in Edinburgh I would have developed a thick skin for dealing with life's little quirks. Not so. When the ship arrived in Naples I decided to head for Pompeii. I had to work a morning shift, so by the time I was ready to go ashore my friends had already gone. I found my way to the railway station and using sign language, I managed to buy a ticket and find the correct platform. I settled into the carriage feeling quite pleased with myself.

I was reading my tourist guide when I heard a "Tsk, Tsk" coming from just ahead of me. I looked up. There, on the next seat opposite, was a youth exposing himself! This great "thing" sticking up in the air and the look on the face of this grinning boy, gave me the fright of my life and I fled from the train just as it was pulling out of the station. I ran back to the ship. My friends all thought it was hilarious and eventually I saw the funny side too. I then thought of all the things I should have said or done to this boy.

That evening I happened to be in the right place at the right time and I was included in a party of senior officers being taken ashore for a meal by the ship's agents. We went to D'Angelos, a very posh restaurant on a hill overlooking Naples. It was a warm, balmy evening and we sat on a terrace with a magnificent view of the city and the bay beyond. The food was superb. I have never tasted pasta and pizza as good as that of Naples. The wine flowed and I had a great night. The Deputy Purser, a rather dour man who, although his office was adjacent to the telephone exchange, never acknowledged the presence of the telephonists, sat next to me and was very friendly all night. He got drunk and became human!

Going ashore in Corfu, the ship's launch deposited us on the quay and my friends and I made our way along the deserted main street looking for some sign of life. We failed to find it. Wandering through narrow cobbled streets where window boxes overflowed with colourful geraniums and cats lay basking in the warm sunshine, we found a café where we sat and enjoyed the peace and quiet, although we would have settled for a bit more action. A taxi deposited us a few miles out of town at a house where the Durrell family once lived. It was now a casino and although it was closed for business, the building was wide open and we were able to wander through the empty rooms at our leisure. There was no-one about. On returning to Corfu on holiday in the 1990s, I failed to recognise anything of the beautiful, sleepy island I once visited.

Boat drill was held on board every week and attendance was compulsory unless you were sleeping after night shift. When the alarm bells sounded crew members had to make their way to a designated boat station, wearing a life-belt and in full uniform, including hat. I hated my "pancake" hat and sometimes I "forgot" to take it with me, getting a telling-off from the inspecting officer. One day I shivered on deck as the wind howled and the ship laboured through heavy seas. I wondered if my hat could blow away in the wind and was surprised how easily it disappeared.

Cabin inspection, known as "Peak Day", was also carried out once a week by the Purser and a senior officer, and cabins had to be spotless. One purser was known to run his finger across the top of the wardrobe. He wasn't averse to opening the wardrobe door on occasion and commenting on the tidiness or otherwise of the interior.

At the end of *Iberia*'s Mediterranean cruising, one of the bell-boys was taken off to jail for starting two fires on board while the ship was in port. He also admitted starting about a dozen of the other fires we had had on board during the previous six months' trip. He was the self-same bell-boy who had been commended by the Captain for alerting the bridge and tackling one of the fires.

When the last cruise to the Mediterranean ended on 6th September, I had a week's leave at home in Rosemarkie, then it was time to re-join *Iberia* for a round-the-world trip, this time to Australia via South Africa and home by the Panama Canal.

Part 3

Round the World 1

*Tilbury to Sydney via the Cape of Good Hope
and Sydney to Tilbury via the Panama Canal
September 1969 to December 1969*

The 16th of September 1969 was cold and dreich as *Iberia* made her way out of Tilbury at the start of our voyage to the southern hemisphere. Our first port of call was Rotterdam, where we embarked another batch of Dutch families heading for a better life in South Africa or Australia.

Janet, my cabin mate was easy to get along with. She liked fine dining, and as she was friendly with one of the chefs, she often got special treatment. We collected from the galley, salmon, seafood and steak, all a feature of the first class menu, but not always on the second class menu, and definitely not on the menu for the crew.

By the time we reached Dakar it was scorching! The quay bristled with stalls offering for sale leatherwork, wood carvings, silver and souvenirs. I admired two beautifully carved ebony heads. "Ten pounds for the two," said the statuesque ebony stallholder. "Nothing less, I have a living to make." It was more than I could afford. I tried bargaining, but I was a novice and my feeble attempts were treated with scorn.

"Try selling some old clothes or some soap," said a helpful engineer, showing me a bath towel and a packet of the ship's best buttermilk bars stuffed under his boilersuit. "They'll sell you anything for soap."

Armed with two white cotton shirts that were too small for me and a bath-size bar of Camay, I tried again: "two shirts, a bar of soap and £3; how about that?" I asked timidly. I thought I detected a flicker of interest. The stall holder examined the shirts carefully. He had already pocketed the soap. "OK. It's a deal." I was pleased with my purchase. The ebony heads were much admired, but would feature strongly in my life when my family suffered a series of unfortunate incidents. But more of that later.

Shortly after leaving Dakar, we had yet another burial at sea, the third during my time on Iberia. The Yeoman of the Mails, a man of forty-six from Tain in Ross-shire, collapsed and died of a heart attack. Just as the sun was setting, with the ship travelling slowly, the burial party formed on the after deck, the body already sewn into a tarpaulin and weighed down with a metal bar. The Captain conducted a short committal service and the body was consigned to the deep with a splash. It looked decidedly final, but I thought it was a strangely comforting end for a mariner.

One day Zigi, the ship's hairdresser asked me if I wanted a job. I had plenty time off so I became a hair-washer in the first class salon. I worked for a few hours almost every day and got 1/6 (7½p) for every head I shampooed. The tips however, were much more generous than the wages and I did quite well out of my part-time post.

I loved it when *Iberia* happened to be in port with one of the other P&O ships, and when we reached Durban, *Orsova* was in the adjoining berth. There began a lot of coming-and-going between the crews of both ships as people contacted friends and arranged to meet over a few drinks. This activity could be at the expense of sightseeing, which I was keen to avoid, but with limited time off, I had to create a balance. I had met Wendy when she was on stand-by in Tilbury and I was keen to hear how she was faring. We combined a chat and catch-up with a trip ashore, which was perfect.

On our journey across the Indian Ocean, we had an emergency on board. The Third Chef had celebrated a little too much on his shore leave in Durban and had a nasty fall on a gangway in the crew quarters. His friends, also inebriated, simply put him to bed. In the morning the man couldn't be roused and the doctor was summoned.

I was on duty in the telephone exchange when the surgeon asked me to contact the carpenter and ask him to bring to the surgery, right away, a brace and a set of bits. For the next two hours or so, hove-to in the heaving seas, stabilisers fully extended, the Captain tried to keep the ship steady while the delicate operation of entering the injured man's brain to relieve the pressure, could be carried out. The operation completed successfully, the ship turned around and went full steam ahead for Durban where a medical team waited on the quay to transfer the man to hospital. The injured man went on to make a complete recovery. The surgeon, Mike Cowen, was hailed a hero by the passengers and crew alike, but he found the praise being heaped on him embarrassing, and opted to stay in his cabin for a few days until everything calmed down.

It was also while crossing the Indian Ocean, that I experienced the worst weather so far in my time at sea. I didn't suffer from seasickness, no matter how bad the weather, which was just as well, as my cabin was situated in the after end of the ship, directly above the propellers. Each time the ship descended into a trough, *Iberia*'s twin propellers were raised out of the water and the noise generated was horrendous. I was kept awake most of the night, and it was a relief to go on duty at six o'clock next morning. On the positive side, the dreaded boat drill was cancelled next day because it was too dangerous to go on deck.

Returning to all the ports that I had visited on my first voyage to Australia, gave me the opportunity to see the sights I had missed on my previous visit. I went ashore at them all and had a second trip to places such as Table Mountain, Fremantle, Adelaide and Melbourne.

We had four days in Sydney before the start of our journey up the Pacific to Hawaii, North America and through the Panama Canal. According to my diary, I spent the time going to the beach, the theatre, ten-pin bowling and shopping, plus I enjoyed just sitting in one or other of Sydney's many parks.

While we were at sea travelling between Suva and Pago Pago, a fire started in the engine room. I thought, "Here we go again!", but this fire was real, not the result of a fire-raiser. It was a huge blaze and took the ship's fire-fighting teams a few hours to extinguish. The seat of the fire was in one of the boilers where paint and lagging went up in flames. A large amount of electrical equipment was burnt and speed was down to a snail's pace. It was impossible to distil any water so supplies were kept for drinking, and the laundry had to be shut down. For three days there was no air-conditioning. It couldn't have happened at a worse time as we were travelling around Fiji and Samoa where the humidity was high. Perspiration ran from every pore even if you didn't move a muscle, and the crew were issued with salt tablets.

The electricians and engineers worked double shifts to try to get things going again, but some of us were secretly hoping they might not be too successful as the prospect of a few days in Honolulu was tempting. The Americans were very strict regarding safety, but on this occasion they were satisfied that the ship was in good condition and we could continue our journey after just one day.

It was my first visit to Vancouver and I was on night duty. *Iberia* was travelling at a snail's pace up Queen Charlotte Strait, the stretch of water that separates Vancouver Island from British Columbia, when the Nightwatchman came to the telephone exchange and offered to watch the switchboard while I went on deck to smell the pines. The perfume was heady. It was a cold, crisp, still night, with not a sound but the gentle throb of the engines and I drank it all in, in the five or so minutes that I spent there.

Because of my duties I only had two-and-a-half hours in Vancouver, enough time for a walk in Stanley Park and a quick tour of the shops. Sailing out of Vancouver was spectacular as we made our stately way under the Lion's Gate Bridge. The peaks of the mountains surrounding the city were snow-covered.

I loved San Francisco. When I went to sea, I said I wanted to see Hong Kong and San Francisco and I was lucky enough to see them both. We had one-and-a-half days in San Francisco, plenty time for me to visit Fisherman's Wharf and ride the famous cable cars.

Fisherman's Wharf teemed with stalls selling live crabs, lobsters and other fish. Janet and I sampled freshly-boiled lobster and crab and wandered round the quaint little shops that inhabited the area. We found an Irish pub and stopped there for a much needed cold drink before heading back to the ship for switchboard duty.

I was up early next morning and wandered in the warm sunshine, through the docks to Fisherman's Wharf. It was here that I saw The Flying Scotsman, the steam train that once plied between London and Edinburgh, lying in a San Francisco siding. It looked rusty and neglected so every time I passed it I gave it a wee pat and assured it that it wasn't forgotten and hopefully someone would rescue it soon.

The Flying Scotsman was built in Doncaster in 1923 and was named after the route of that name: the London and Edinburgh Flying Scotsman Train Service. When the engine was withdrawn from service in January 1963, it was bought by a private investor who took it to America with the intention of carrying out an extensive tour of America and Canada. The engine was left to deteriorate however, when the owner ran out of money, and the Flying Scotsman was seized by creditors. Sir William McAlpine, businessman and rail enthusiast, eventually bought the engine for £25,000, paid off the creditors and shipped it back to the UK, where it was restored. It went on to tour Australia in 1988/89. In 2016 the engine was given a total refit and placed in Doncaster Museum. The engine occasionally comes out of retirement to carry out a few journeys up and down the country carrying train enthusiasts and people who are happy to recall the great days of steam.

My work pattern allowed me a few hours in Los Angeles, so I went with an engineer friend to Marineland. The stars of the demonstration of fishy antics were Bubbles the Whale and Flipper the Dolphin. Our one-and-a-half hours were not enough to appreciate the many specimens of marine life that were on display here, but I had to get back to the ship in time for my next shift. On the way we saw the great orange ball of the sun sink slowly into the calm mirror of the sea: a wonderful sight.

Acapulco was just a sleepy town in the sixties and I loved it. The ship anchored in Acapulco Bay and we were ferried ashore by the ship's tenders. A group of us went water ski-ing, but I was so hopeless at it that I gave up and sat in the towing boat while the others triumphed.

The Hotel El Mirador was our next stop, where we relaxed on a terrace overlooking the spot where the cliff divers gave displays for the tourists. These young men dive from a height of about 120 feet into a narrow channel, timing their dive with the incoming waves so that there is enough water to prevent them hitting the bottom. After completing their spectacular dives, they came to the hotel courtyard looking for money from the tourists. If they were lucky the hotel staff turned a blind eye, but sometimes they sent the boys packing.

Transiting the Panama Canal was a wonderful experience and I spent the time viewing it from the hospital deck. As we traversed the Gaillard Cut, a four-hour journey through dense tropical vegetation and steep cliffs rising to three times the height of *Iberia*'s mast, we looked out for crocodiles. According to the port notes, crocodiles could be seen basking in the sun, but with several pairs of eyes trained on the shore, we failed to see any. We did, however, see a crocodile as we traversed Gatun Lake, an entirely man-made lake in the highest part of the canal. Halfway across the lake lay Barro Colorado Island which contained an internationally famous wildlife sanctuary. Gatun Lake was formed by damming the Chagres River, and the numerous small islands one sees are actually the tops of the hills in the original state of the area.

We arrived at Cristobal, at the eastern end of the Panama Canal at six o'clock in the evening, and with just enough time for the disembarkation of passengers before our departure three hours later, no shore leave was allowed.

The weather in Curacao, our next stop, was hot. This was normally a port where we anchored off and went ashore by launch, but there was a problem with Iberia's engines. The starboard engine couldn't be turned off, so for safety reasons, we tied up at a tanker berth.

I went ashore for the day with Alison and when we arrived back on board for the start of my shift at five o'clock that evening, there was pandemonium and a strong smell of oil. As the ship was being refuelled, a fuel tank blew out under pressure and spilled thick black oil over everything in the first class baggage room. The Purser's department had the sorry task of inviting passengers to

Acapulco cliff divers at El Mirador Hotel.

identify their belongings. Wedding presents, furniture, fur coats, documents and various other items were being recorded for compensation purposes. The rest of the voyage was not very pleasant as the smell of the oil lingered in spite of thorough cleaning.

As with most things, conspiracy theories abounded, and rumour on the ship was that the boilermaker, who was supervising the refuelling operation, fell asleep and when the pipeline slipped, he didn't notice until the damage was done.

The atmosphere, hustle and bustle, the noise and the smells of the town of Bridgetown, Barbados were very inviting and I went ashore with Janet. Janet's idea of a trip ashore in Bridgetown however, meant a visit to all the posh hotels in the town, which she

Transiting the Panama Canal.

seemed to know intimately. Janet introduced me to rum punch: delicious but lethal. When Janet went back on board to start her shift, I wandered through the teeming streets, just looking and soaking up the atmosphere. A swim in the crystal clear water followed, after which I sat on the silver sands with my book for a couple of hours. Going ashore again in the evening, I found Bridgetown to be even more beautiful when darkness fell. The sound of steel bands blared from every bar. My friends and I had a meal of spicy seafood at a beachside restaurant and danced to a fabulous steel band. It was hard to drag ourselves away for sailing at midnight.

Our six days crossing the Atlantic were spent catching up on sleep and getting ready for our end-of-voyage leave. I was heading home to Rosemarkie as I had decided to take a few months off. Homesickness was still bothering me. I thought a period at home with my family would do me the world of good and bring me back down to earth.

We celebrated St Andrew's Day mid-Atlantic and I introduced Janet and a few others to the delights of haggis (courtesy of the ship's friendly Scots chef), bashed neeps and mash, washed down with whisky. Accompanied by the songs and poems of Rabbie Burns, it was great fun.

When we reached Southampton, it was pandemonium as we disembarked passengers and cargo, and got the standby crews settled in. I had a few days in Bristol, then I went on to Bishop Auckland to the wedding of the Nursing Sister, Dora and Radio Officer Gordon, who had only disembarked themselves a few days previously. We entered the church in the middle of a snowstorm, but the weather didn't dampen our spirits and a good time was had by all. Next day I headed north. This was my last trip on *Iberia*. I spent Christmas and New Year with my family and then set about looking for a job ashore.

Part 4

On the Home Front

December 1969 to December 1971

During three months at home, I looked around for suitable jobs. One interview was for the post of tele-printer operator in Air Traffic Control at the airport at Croydon, the forerunner of Heathrow. I couldn't type, but at my interview at Edinburgh I passed the typing test and was told I was suitable. After a few days at home however, I didn't feel confident enough to carry out a job where accuracy was crucial, so I turned it down. This is one of the very few regrets I have as on second thoughts I'm sure I could have coped. I would also have liked to have spent some time in London.

After three months in an accountants' office in Inverness, I was bored, so I started applying for jobs in Edinburgh. I managed to get an interview at the Western General Hospital where they were looking for typists. I still couldn't type, but after the interview I agreed to take a typing test. From her seat in the reception area, my friend Sheila, who had accompanied me, sat squirming with embarrassment as she heard my slow tap, tap, tapping on the typewriter. When I emerged from the office, she was doubled up, tears of laughter streaming down her face. "I don't think you'll get *that* job" was all she said. I got it.

A couple of weeks into my new job in the Haematology Lab at the Western General, I developed rheumatic pains in my knees, which swelled to the size of small footballs. Soon after, my hands did likewise. I was in a lot of pain, and the medication in those days was a high dose of soluble aspirin. My boss sent me to his friend, the consultant in charge of the Rheumatology Unit at the Northern General Hospital. Exercise, change of diet, rest, nothing helped.

At home, my family began to suffer several misfortunes. My mother developed pleurisy and was very ill for a few weeks. My brother, on exercises aboard a submarine in the Atlantic, was smitten by a mysterious illness which deprived him of the use of his legs. A mercy dash to hospital in Gibraltar saved his life. Then my aunt suffered a stroke and my cousin was involved in a car accident; my nephew was rushed to hospital with suspected meningitis. A deep depression settled over the family.

One day, home in Rosemarkie for the weekend, my eyes were attracted to the ebony heads I had purchased in Dakar in 1969 and which had pride of place on my mother's living-room wall. A sudden chill ran up my spine. Beautiful as they were, I couldn't get it out of my mind that they had something to do with the run of misfortune plaguing the family. They would have to go. I wrapped them in newspaper and put them in the dustbin.

Next day the hospital rang to say that my nephew was out of danger. We were overjoyed. Both my aunt and my cousin went on to recover enough to lead fairly normal lives, and my mother also recovered her health. A few weeks later my brother arrived home unexpectedly, looking fit and well. He presented Mother with a huge bunch of golden daffodils. The long winter had come to an end, together with our mysterious run of misfortune.

After a year working in the lab, my rheumatism was still bothering me and my social life was being drastically curtailed. My Edinburgh GP said to me one day, "Get away back to sea lassie. The heat will do you good." I took his advice, and exactly two years since I left the sea, I was heading for Southampton.

On 8th December 1971, I boarded SS Canberra for the first of several spells of "Standby". Over the next few months, *Orcades, Oriana, Oronsay, Chusan* and *Himalaya* arrived in Southampton, now the home port for all P&O vessels.

"Standby" was the term used for the duties carried out by the temporary crews who took over the ships when the regular crews were on shore leave. The spells on standby could be for a few days or they could last for several weeks if the ship was in dry dock. Nowadays, no-one would tolerate the deprivation the standby crews had to put up with when the ships went into dry dock for repair. We still lived on board and had no hot water, no light and no hot food so many trips were made to the local swimming baths for a shower. We lived on fish and chips and Chinese takeaways and spent a fortune on hairdos. As compensation however, there was a lot of socialising with staff from the other P&O ships berthed nearby. The strict separation of officers and crew didn't exist in dock and everyone mixed freely. I met up with a few of my old shipmates from *Iberia* and it was nice just to slip back into the routine of life on board a ship.

Part 5

A New Ship and
Mediterranean Cruising

April 1972 to May 1972

Orsova arrived in Southampton on 6th April 1972 and I heard there was a vacancy for a telephonist on board. After four months on standby I was ready to go to sea and I was delighted to be appointed to *Orsova*. She was soon to embark on two Mediterranean cruises before heading off on a trip round the world.

My cabin mate was Ros who had been to sea for a few years and knew the ropes. Ros complained all the time about everything and anything and could have been difficult, but we managed to get along companionably, as long as we each kept our distance. Ros suffered from a bad back and slept on the day bed rather than her bunk, so when she was sleeping after her night shift, I had to find somewhere else to sit. The telephonists were allowed to use the passenger decks as long as they were discreet and I often found a quiet corner in which to settle down with my book or my knitting. When it was too cold to sit on deck, I sometimes borrowed the key to an empty cabin, courtesy of a friendly cabin steward. I used the well-stocked library in the first class section of the ship, visiting it in the middle of the night when it was deserted and there was less chance of being seen.

One drawback of sailing on *Orsova* was that the telephonists ate in the leading hands' mess, not in the passenger dining-room as we did on *Iberia*. I didn't like it. The food was fine, but the mess was noisy, crowded and smelt of grease and smoke. After two weeks I could stand it no more and arranged an interview with the Purser, when I asked if the Telephonists could eat in the Tourist dining-room. I mentioned that *Iberia* already allowed this. My argument was obviously sound and the telephonists and steward-esses were given a table in the Tourist dining-room.

Modern cruising means being in a port every day, but in the six-ties we enjoyed long leisurely days at sea. Passengers played deck quoits and table tennis, swam in the pool, read a book and enjoyed being pampered by the many waiters mingling with their trays of cold soft drinks, all free of charge.

Entertainment was provided in the evening by a few low-key professionals: a motley band cobbled together from a selection of individual musicians and supplemented by the crew, mainly offi-cers, who were only too glad to have something to do other than prop up the bars. The Entertainments Officer, assisted by two Social Hostesses, one in First Class and one in Tourist, organised the evening programmes. Noreen was the Hostess in Tourist Class, and befriended me soon after we sailed. She too, was to be my entry into the officer social round and after three days on board she invited me to a drinks party in her cabin where I met the Staff Captain, the First Officer and several other senior officers, includ-ing the Entertainments Officer. Alison, the Senior Nursing Sister was also on board, so my connection with the Medical Staff was re-established.

Our first port on the short Mediterranean cruise was Funchal in Madeira where we were staying overnight. I was delighted to get ashore and throw myself into sightseeing again. A group of us took a bus to Monte to the restaurant with the best view in Madeira and which I had visited previously. After a lunch of barbecued meat served on a skewer hanging from a hook in the ceiling and tasting delicious, my companions and I took a toboggan ride back to the town over the smooth round cobbles of the old roadway. The length of the run is three-and-a-quarter miles and takes about twenty minutes to negotiate and it was an exhilarating experience.

Madeira is famous for its embroidery, its wickerwork and its flowers and we came upon an open-air market which sold all of these things. It was full of passengers from the ship who seemed to be having a buying frenzy. The short route from the market to the ship was crowded with passengers laden with chairs, baskets and flowers.

Next morning I was up early to see the Royal Yacht *Britannia*, accompanied by a Portuguese submarine arrive in Funchal Harbour. *Britannia* was dressed overall and looked spick and span with her crew standing to attention on the decks. Crowds lined the shore to watch.

Lanzarote was our next port, and I was pleasantly surprised. Some of the crew called it "Grotty Lanzarote" so I wasn't expecting it to be up to much. It was charming. The long walk into town was through a barren landscape dotted with low scrub and rocks. The town looked Moroccan, with low, white-washed buildings and a long esplanade bordered by palm trees. There were flowers everywhere, growing in huge beds and in pots, and every house sported a hanging basket. The sand was black. Tourism was in the very early stages here with just one high-rise hotel on the sea-front, the Grand Hotel where Ros and I had coffee and sat by the swimming pool.

Our call at Tenerife was short, just six hours and as I was on duty I was unable to go sight-seeing. I always made sure I went ashore however, even if it was just a walk along the quay, and this was what I did in Tenerife. The place was deserted, as the ship was docked far from any built-up area.

In Dakar, I joined a tour of the city where we viewed all the important Government buildings, the best Dakar could offer. We also had the obligatory buffet in a rather posh hotel. The second part of the tour however, was to Medina, a shanty-town at the edge of the city. The poverty and deprivation were horrendous and the smell overpowering, but these smiling people had set up a small market stall to sell their home-made trinkets, beads, straw hats and baskets. The passengers were horrified and bought up almost all their stock, simply because they felt sorry for them.

Mediterranean cruising saw the introduction of same-day turn-arounds in Southampton and the first of these turned out to be pretty hectic. Once the passengers had disembarked, the ship was cleaned and the cabins prepared for the next batch of cruisers. Embarkation was always busy with passengers getting lost or looking for directions, usually to the nearest bar, and having a good look into every nook and cranny, including the telephone exchange. Everyone breathed a sigh of relief when we eventually cast off from the wharf and headed down the Solent.

Church services were held every Sunday while the ship was at sea and crew members were encouraged to attend to boost the numbers. If I was off duty I usually went along. The service was taken by the Staff Captain and was pretty much the same each time. We always ended with the naval hymn, "Eternal Father Strong to Save."

On this particular cruise I noted in my diary on the day we sailed, that we had a lot of bad-mannered passengers on board. After three days of rough weather including a horrendous crossing of the Bay of Biscay, their mood didn't improve and we all longed for some sunshine to cheer them up. When we reached Palma, Majorca, the sun shone and the crew breathed a sigh of relief when the tour buses headed for the mountains. As the weather warmed, so did the mood of the passengers.

In Palma I went ashore with Mae, one of the stewardesses and met quite by chance, Bert, a Quartermaster I had sailed with on Iberia, and who was on holiday on the island. He came shopping with us and carried the parcels. When Mae went back to the ship at five o'clock, Bert took me to a wonderful seafood restaurant where we ate lobster paella and shared a bottle of champagne. He then paid for a taxi to get me back to the ship in time for my 8.30 shift. My high-living, exciting life had begun again!

In Malta I was sitting alone in the public gardens overlooking Valetta's Grand Harbour eating my picnic lunch, when I was approached by an old man who began to chat to me about the Second World War and the important role played by Malta during that time.

In the summer of 1942, for 154 days and nights, German and Italian bombs rained down on the island. No ships could reach the island with supplies and the people were on the brink of starvation. He remembered vividly the deprivation endured by the

Maltese during the siege and the great relief and happiness experienced when the people saw the naval relief force limping in. The flotilla had been severely bombed in their effort to reach the island and it was only because of the professionalism of the captains and crews of the ships that they were able to stay afloat long enough to reach their destination. We chatted for about an hour and he walked back to the launch with me. He was an extremely interesting man and I learned a lot about Malta's role in the conflict which resulted in the island being awarded the George Cross.

In October 2017 I attended a lunch aboard *HMS Wellington*, moored alongside the Victoria Embankment at Temple Pier, London. *HMS Wellington*, a Grimsby Class Sloop of 1256 tons built in 1938 and with a sailing history of six years on convoy duties in the Atlantic, was in 1947, purchased by The Honourable Company of Master Mariners to serve as their Livery Hall and Headquarters. The engine and boiler rooms were transformed into large areas suitable for conferences, meetings and receptions, with other parts being made into office space for management, plus a library and gallery for the display of a collection of marine paintings, ship models and other artefacts of maritime significance.

In the gallery I noticed a painting of the *SS Ohio*, an American oil tanker requisitioned by the allies to re-supply Malta with oil, and discovered that this was the first ship to enter Valetta Harbour on 15th August 1942, successfully breaking the siege and delivering badly needed fuel to the island. The gentleman who told me about the painting, said that the artist had omitted to include in the picture, two German aircraft that had crashed on to the decks of the *Ohio*, one on the stern and the other on the foredeck. According to Wikipedia, the *Ohio* was abandoned and re-boarded twice on her journey towards Valetta and eventually had to be supported by two Royal Navy destroyers, *HMS Penn* and *HMS Ledbury*, one on either side of her, in an effort to keep her afloat and reach successfully, the safety of Grand Harbour.

As *Ohio* approached her destination, thousands of Maltese men and women crowded the ramparts above the wreck-strewn harbour, waving and cheering, while a brass band played Rule Britannia. Captain Mason, in spite of the urgency and the threat that *Ohio* could still sink, found time to take the salute from *Ohio*'s battered bridge. Mission accomplished, *Ohio* would never sail again.

My one and only trip to the romantic city of Venice was anything but, as it poured rain the whole day and my sightseeing had to be done between showers. St Mark's Square was wonderful however, even under an inch or two of water. An orchestra, huddled under an awning, played on regardless of the deluge. I went into the Patriarchal Cathedral Basilica of St Mark, also known as St Mark's Basilica, next to the Doge's Palace in St Mark's Square. In my diary I describe the interior as being fabulous, but unfortunately I don't say why. I do mention, however, the beautiful jewelled screen which took my breath away. The Rialto Bridge was also on my itinerary and I strolled through the markets nearby, enjoying a coffee at one of the many outdoor cafés in a brief spell of sunshine between showers.

Some of the crew had a more exciting time ashore, it would appear. Harold the Projectionist got hopelessly drunk, and on duty that evening, showed a film, Steptoe and Son, back to front. There were very few in the audience and they let it run for quite some time before one of the passengers got a bit fed up and reported it to the Purser's department. Harold got a ticking off.

Messina was a bit of a let-down. I went ashore with a couple of companions but parted company with them soon after as they weren't interested in sightseeing. I visited the cathedral, but I was molested at every turn and was pleased when I bumped into some of the bureau staff. We took a taxi to the Lido but as it was a public holiday, everything had closed, including the public beach. The weather was pretty awful and our departure, scheduled for six o'clock that evening, was delayed because of the high winds. We sailed at six the next morning.

Because of our extra twelve hours' stay at Messina, the Captain decided to give the next scheduled port, Alicante, a miss and we headed straight for Gibraltar. The weather deteriorated and so did the mood of the passengers and the complaints started again. Our stay in Gibraltar was short and I didn't manage to get ashore.

It was at the First Class Casino Night that I fell out with one of the stewardesses when I saw her pocketing a pound note from the takings. We only made £9 the whole evening as the passengers, even the first class ones, weren't very generous. I resolved to keep an eye on her in future, but I was spared this, as she decided not to take part in any more themed evenings and left the ship when we reached Southampton.

In Lisbon, our last port before Southampton, I went ashore early in the morning with one escudo in my purse, so my sightseeing was done on foot. I walked to Belem to see the statue to Henry the Navigator. Henry was a Portuguese prince who was born in 1394 and was noted for his patronage of voyages of discovery, although his title of Henry the Navigator is a misnomer as he never did undertake any voyages of discovery himself. A walk through some gardens and a cup of coffee costing one escudo, passed the time until I returned to the ship for my next stint on duty at 12.30.

The cruise ended as it had started: with some disgruntled passengers. The weather had been pretty poor and the few days of sunny weather hadn't lifted their mood. It was just as well that this was the last Mediterranean Cruise for *Orsova* before heading off to the southern hemisphere for a few months. I was travelling home to Rosemarkie for my first longish leave in six months and was looking forward to seeing the family again.

Part 6

Round the World 2

Southampton to Sydney via the Panama Canal and Sydney to Southampton via the Cape of Good Hope May 1972 to October 1972

After ten days at home in Rosemarkie, it was back on board *Orsova*. I was excited at the prospect of another round-the-world trip. This one was going to a few ports I had not yet visited. We were heading west through the Panama Canal to Australia and home via South Africa.

We had a few days in Southampton before the start of the voyage. The ship was berthed quite a distance from the city centre, but on reading my diary, I find that I was good at getting free lifts from members of the crew hiring taxis, or with some of the crew who had their cars parked nearby.

Southampton was fairly small in the 1970s and we were always bumping into someone we knew. One entry in my diary reads: "Went ashore in the evening with Viv (hostess) and got a lift in a taxi hired by the welfare officer, Welfare Willie. He was going to a pub and bought us a drink before we headed off to the cinema. At the interval we met Martin and he also treated us to a drink. After the film we went to a nearby pub and met up with Welfare Willie again, who treated us to a meal before taking us back to the ship in a taxi." A cheap evening out for us it would appear.

We sailed at six o'clock the following afternoon and I watched from the comfort of the hospital deck. The weather forecast was poor and it remained cold and grey for a few days. This didn't suit the passengers, who became a bit demanding. Very few of them turned out for the Casino nights and our takings in the Tourist section came to 91p and in the first class section, £1.91.

After six days crossing the Atlantic, Hamilton, Bermuda was our first port of call. We embarked our pilot off St David's Head at the east end of Bermuda, and travelled slowly along the entire north coast of the islands, through The Narrows and the quaintly named Five Fathom Hole, towards our anchorage at Grassy Bay.

Bermuda takes its name from the Spanish navigator, Juan Bermudez, who visited the islands in 1515 and claimed them for the Spanish Empire. They remained uninhabited however, until 1609 when Admiral Sir George Somers' ship *Sea Venturer*, was wrecked on the reefs surrounding the islands. Sir George had been escorting a convoy carrying settlers from Britain. They were named the Somers Islands after Sir George, but later, the earlier name of Bermuda was re-adopted.

Although it was dull and wet, the islands looked green and inviting. I was disappointed not to be able to go ashore immediately, as I drew the short straw and had to work all day. The next day however, I was up early and caught the first tender ashore. My friends and I got on the local bus to Somerset, the most westerly village on the island and reputedly the most scenic. We weren't disappointed. We passed beautiful beaches of silver sand and turquoise water, the best I'd ever seen, but we didn't have time to linger as I had to be back on board for the start of my shift at 12.30 that afternoon. We sailed at four.

Port Everglades in 1972 was a flat swamp forty miles from Miami Beach. Here we embarked four hundred American passengers and the ship's crew had to undertake a very strict boat drill under the eyes of the US port authorities. The American passengers were also much more demanding than our normal run of passengers and were constantly making phone calls and requesting all sorts of services which we had to try and provide instantly. The laundry staff were kept busy, as well as the galley staff, with meals being served in the cabins out-with normal mealtimes. We were all told however, that the Americans had to be catered for as they were important customers. Until the majority of American passengers disembarked in San Francisco twelve days later, the telephonists were kept busy: all the telephonists were on short shifts of two hours at a time during our two-day stay in Port Everglades when things got a bit hectic.

It was during the journey between Port Everglades and San Francisco that I met an interesting American passenger. Most nights when I was off duty, I went up on deck just to lean on the ship's rail and look at the stars. The elderly American gentleman joined me at the rail one evening and we had a long interesting conversation discussing anything and everything. Several times during the next 12 days I would take my place at the ship's rail, and soon after I'd be joined by my new friend, when we'd carry on where we left off, wondering if we really were the only inhabited planet in the universe (highly unlikely we decided, on the evidence above our heads) and were we really made in six days (ie: was there a God? Unresolved). On our last meeting the night before we docked at San Francisco, he gave me his card and said if I ever decided to visit America, there would be a job for me with his company. Visiting America wasn't part of my plan however, and I didn't take him up on his offer.

Nassau, the capital of the Bahamas, was our next port of call and I was able to go ashore for the whole eight hours of our stay there. It was Sunday, and Alison and I treated ourselves to coffee and muffins at the Sheraton British Colonial Hotel, a colossal edifice overlooking the harbour. It was built in the colonial style both inside and outside, and had a reputation for elegance and style, as well as being hugely expensive.

Our next stop was to the Scots Kirk where we heard a lovely children's service which included a christening. We sat at the back of the church and were quite amused when it came to the naming of the child. I can't remember the actual names, but the list was similar to the following: "I name you Angus, Duncan, Farquhar, MacDonald, Fergus, Calum, Hamish, MacPherson," and on and on and on. The poor wee mite had at least ten names. We had the chance to meet the recipient of the string of Scottish names at the tea and cakes served in the church garden afterwards. We also met the minister of the kirk who, although being Bahamas-born, had a wonderful Scots accent.

Nassau was holding a straw market that day, and we spent quite some time strolling round the stalls laden with beautiful, colourful straw hats, baskets and other odds and ends. It was fascinating to watch many of the articles actually being made by the industrious stallholders as they sat at their stalls chatting and laughing with each other. It was a happy place and our visit there finished off the day nicely.

My second trip through the Panama Canal was from east to west. I spent several hours on deck enjoying the silence of it all. Even the engines were inaudible as we slowly traversed the various lakes and stretches of smooth water. Hundreds of colourful butterflies and large dragonflies abounded, while flocks of vultures wheeled overhead.

This artificial waterway connects the Atlantic and Pacific Oceans and at 48 miles long and rising ninety feet to the highest point before descending to sea level at the other end, the canal is a magnificent effort of engineering and was many years in the planning and construction. France began work on the canal in 1881 but had to abandon the project due to engineering problems and a high mortality rate. Labelled the largest and most difficult engineering project ever undertaken, work resumed in 1904 when the United States stepped in to complete the canal. The work took ten years and in January 1914 it was eventually opened to traffic.

I never failed to enjoy watching the "mules" as the electric locomotives were called, gently guiding the ship through the narrow locks where there was very little room between the ship and the massive sides of the lock. Lines were attached from the ship to four huge mechanical "mules": two at the bow and two at the stern. These "mules" trundled back and forth, grunting and squeaking as our great white liner was nudged into each lock with barely an inch to spare. Apparently great skill is required by the operators of these locomotives and the men undergo an extensive training.

Acapulco was the next stop and it was hot. After wandering around the town on my own looking at the shops, I fell in with Allan, the ship's surgeon who was also at a loose end. We strolled round the market and admired the many stalls selling precious

Panama Canal Mule.

and semi-precious stones, especially emeralds. We were tempted to buy, but the prices asked didn't really reflect the true cost of the gems and we decided that most of them were probably fake. I had to work in the evening, but as we sailed out of Acapulco Bay at two o'clock next morning, I stood on deck and enjoyed watching the lights of the town fade into the distance. It was a clear night and the stars were so amazing that I couldn't tear myself away, and stayed on deck much longer than I intended.

In Los Angeles, Rita worked my shift and I was able to have a whole day off. Six of us, Alison, Noreen, Claire, Maggie, Allan and I were on the first bus away from the ship heading for Disneyland, my first visit there. Advertised as "The Happiest Place on Earth,"

I thought it was wonderful. I marvelled at the Pirates of the Caribbean, sang along to the Bears Jamboree, screamed in the Haunted House, rode the Santa Fe and Disneyland Railroad, visited the Swiss Family Robinson and chatted to Mickey Mouse and Pluto. Tired and happy, we got the last bus back to the ship before we sailed at six o'clock that evening

Next stop was San Francisco and we were there for three days. Several telephone landlines were attached to the ship and the American passengers were not slow to take advantage. The ship's agents also kept the telephonists busy as they ordered supplies or queried orders. The telephonists were responsible for sending out telephone accounts to the passengers and it was important to time all calls and ensure the accounts were sent to the right person. Some of these calls ran into hundreds of dollars and we were in deep trouble if we got anything wrong.

San Francisco in the seventies was a wonderful place, and safe for a single female to wander. At least I think it was. I did it several times and never came to any harm. I rode the cable cars and enjoyed the view of Alcatraz, the prison lying in the middle of San Francisco Bay. On one of these solo sightseeing forays, I visited Lombard Street, known as "the crookedest street in the world." It had eight tight hairpin bends in the short quarter mile length and was open to one-way traffic only, travelling downhill.

I visited The Cannery, a massive shopping-centre-cum-market-place which had been built on the site of the old Del Monte fruit cannery. It comprised shops, arcades, open walkways, courtyards with huge trees and shrubs and it was a very pleasant place to spend a couple of hours browsing and relaxing in one of the many cafes and seated areas. Soft music and hushed voices added to the quiet ambience.

Going out for breakfast is a great American tradition, so some friends and I tried it. You need to have the capacity for large meals, as American portions are stupendous. I was surprised the first time I breakfasted ashore and had bacon and eggs with pancakes. My delicious breakfast was suddenly doused in maple syrup.

It was in San Francisco that Ros and I were taken out for a meal by Bob the Plumber and Harold the Projectionist, two old bachelors who had been to sea for years and were inseparable. We were

Bob and Harold.

taken to Ginsberg's, an Irish pub which, we were told, was a favourite haunt of the stars, but we didn't recognise any that night. It was on to The Rusty Scupper, which despite its name was a very upmarket seafood restaurant, where we had a fantastic meal of the most wonderful seafood. Bob and Harold's reputation as two die-hard old drunks was shattered that night as they returned to the ship in a fairly sober state, having walked all the way, a distance of about four miles.

On my last day in San Francisco, I went ashore with Ann, one of the telephonists from *Oronsay* which was berthed next to us, and had a wonderful seafood lunch at Fisherman's Wharf followed by a cable-car ride to Chinatown. It was wonderful just strolling around, window-shopping and people-watching.

Vancouver was our next stop and I managed to get on a tour to Grouse Mountain. The weather was so awful however, that we could see nothing because of the mist and I was glad I hadn't paid for the tour. The passengers complained. The cold weather continued and next day we all nearly froze on boat drill which seemed to take much longer than usual.

After a couple of days steaming westwards, the weather began to improve and three days later we were into "whites." This was when we exchanged the navy blue suit and collar and tie for a white dress and shoes.

We arrived at Honolulu at nine o'clock in the morning two days later and Maggie Pile (children's hostess) and I were off the ship as soon as the gangway was lowered, heading for the Ala Moana shopping centre, situated about two miles from our berth in Honolulu Harbour. The Ala Moana centre was, according to my port notes, one of the largest in the world and the best place to buy Hawaiian outfits at reasonable prices. Spoiled for choice, Maggie and I took our time trawling the stores and each bought a muu-muu (a loose dress which hangs from the shoulder, traditionally worn in Hawaii) and a pair of sandals. We were both heading out that night for what we hoped would be memorable, romantic occasions in Honolulu.

That night, wearing my new muu-muu and sandals, I was wined and dined ashore. My date was waiting on the quay with a garland of fragrant frangipani, known as a "lei". This is presented and draped round the neck of all visitors arriving or leaving the Hawaiian Islands. The perfume was heady and together with the balmy night air, the smell of steaks sizzling on barbecues and the sound of twangy Hawaiian guitars, it made for a wonderful experience. I was treated to champagne and fine food at a very upmarket restaurant in Honolulu. After dinner, we sat around a glass-topped piano drinking coffee and listening to music.

Honolulu, capital city of America's fiftieth state, is located on the island of Oahu, third largest of the island chain of eight major islands (seven of which are inhabited) in the Hawaiian group. The islands lie more than two thousand miles in any direction from a "mainland" or large land mass and cover an area of 6,400 square miles. According to my port notes of 1972, the population of the islands at that time was over 700,000, of whom about 600,000 lived on Oahu.

The production of sugar, which began in a small way around 1802, grew in importance and in 1972 Hawaii was producing an annual sugar crop of over a million tons. By 1882 the first pineapple plantations were begun and by the 1960s, 80% of the world's output of canned pineapple was being exported from Hawaii.

Our knowledge of the history of the Hawaiian Islands doesn't start until the landing of Captain James Cook on 18th January 1778 when he named the islands the Sandwich Islands in honour of his patron the Earl of Sandwich. On his return to the islands the following year however, Captain Cook was killed by the natives in a skirmish over the theft of one of his ship's boats.

Captain George Vancouver, a British officer of the Royal Navy, made two visits to the islands in 1792 and 1794 while in command of the newly-launched HMS Discovery. Vancouver had a good rapport with the natives of Hawaii, and in 1794 he took possession of the islands in the name of King George III, with the agreement of King Kamehameha. This action however, was never ratified by the British Government and in 1898 Hawaii became a territory of the United States. On 12th March 1959 Hawaii was named the fiftieth state of the United States of America.

When you became ill on board, taking the day off and spending it in bed meant that others had to work extra to cover your shift. I always tried hard to keep going no matter how bad I felt. When I woke up the day after we sailed from Honolulu, I had a raging sore throat, dry gritty eyes and a temperature. I had to crawl out of bed to start my duty at six o'clock that morning. Bob the Plumber knew exactly what I needed however, and came to the cabin at lunchtime with a large shot of Southern Comfort which I converted into a hot toddy, went back to bed and woke up in time for my evening shift as right as rain.

A short visit to Suva gave me time to go ashore with Alison to the Travelodge Hotel for breakfast of paw-paw, French toast with cinnamon and syrup, and coffee. There were few holiday-makers around in Fiji in 1972 and the passengers from the ship tended to go outwith the town for their sightseeing, so we shared the hotel lounge with perhaps two or three couples at most. We enjoyed strolling through the market where we admired and sometimes bought, odd-looking fruits that we normally never saw anywhere else.

I was still enjoying taking part in all the on-board activities that allowed me access to the passenger decks and my appearance there was by now taken as normal. We had just had a Wild West Casino Night where I manned the Tombola table with Mona, one of the children's hostesses. The passengers weren't great spenders and we made the magnificent sum of £17. Now I was in the throes of preparing for Old-Tyme Music Hall where I was the wardrobe mistress.

In Auckland I went on a morning tour of the city which included a trip to the zoo. The weather was awful: wet and windy. In the evening, Bob the plumber and Harold the projectionist took me ashore to a pub where we helped ourselves from a whole chicken and a pile of hamburgers plonked down in the middle of the table. Fine dining it was not! My company wasn't interesting enough for Bob and Harold however, as they disappeared early on in the evening and I had to make my own way back to the ship. Luckily the pub wasn't far from our berth and my initial panic receded when I found my bearings and made it safely back without incident.

We had three days at sea before reaching Sydney. The weather was pretty foul and I noted in my diary that the movement of the ship was the worst I'd experienced so far. It had the effect of sending me to sleep and when I was on duty I had to ensure that the night buzzer was switched on so that I didn't miss any calls.

When we reached Sydney, Ros was ill again and Rita and I had to cover for her so there wasn't much time for sightseeing. On the third day I managed to get ashore at seven o'clock in the morning when I walked to the Botanical Gardens, but I couldn't linger as I was back on duty at ten. They were a hard few days and I was shattered. We were supposed to sail on day four, but an oilmen's strike meant our afternoon sailing was cancelled. The upside to this cancellation was however, that I was able to go to the theatre that night to see Jesus Christ Superstar which was showing in Sydney. Next day we sailed and had nine days at sea to look forward to before we reached our next port of call, Hong Kong.

It was great being back in Hong Kong but I narrowly escaped being flown home after one day. The purser on *Orsova* was not a friendly person and he wasn't too keen on the telephonists, having had occasion to haul them over the coals for being rude to passengers. (I was not included in this censure as I took great pride in my job and made sure that passengers came first.) I went out in the company of several officers and as I walked into the Hong Kong Hyatt Hotel, who should be sitting at the bar but the Purser. He was pretty drunk, but not so drunk that he didn't know who I was. We didn't linger in his company and I forgot all about it as I enjoyed my night out in the hotel's restaurant and nightclub. Next morning I was called into the Deputy Purser's office where I was told that the Purser was sending me home. My crime: mixing with officers. I was furious. I asked how many of the officers who were with me were also being sent home, although I already knew the answer. A couple of hours later I was told that the Purser had had second thoughts and I could stay! On hindsight, I think it was just a warning and not a serious consideration. I made sure we all knew where the Purser was in future.

We had three days in Hong Kong and it was here that I preferred to buy my souvenirs and presents to take home. I met up with Noreen and Alison, veteran shoppers who knew the best places to shop. We boarded one of the Star Ferries to Hong Kong Island where Alison led us to a jewellery shop tucked away in a side street. Here I was introduced to Mikimoto pearls.

Mikimoto Kōkichi was a Japanese entrepreneur who is credited with creating the first cultured pearl. He subsequently started the cultured pearl industry with the establishment of his luxury pearl company, Mikimoto. As a boy he watched local fishermen in his home village depositing their treasures on the shore and he began a lifetime's fascination with pearls. It took him many years to perfect the system of obtaining a perfect spherical pearl. This was done by inserting a piece of material into the oyster shell. The oyster created tissue to make a sac over the irritant, thus creating a pearl. When he discovered in 1916 that a Japanese government biologist, Tokichi Nishikawa, had already patented a similar but much easier method of creating a pearl, Mikimoto Kōkichi entered into an arrangement with him and the Mikimoto business began to expand rapidly.

Not all cultured pearls were perfectly formed however, and the misshapen ones, advertised as Baroque, were sold at prices far below that of the perfect version. I was delighted with my eighteen-inch rope of Baroque pearls for which I paid the grand sum of £10.

Next day a group of us headed to the Ocean Terminal where we spent the last of our Hong Kong money. We sailed at midnight, on a warm balmy evening with no disasters befalling the ship. The lights of Hong Kong were superb, like hanging lantern decorations high up the mountains and reaching right down to the sea.

It was my first visit to Japan and I was looking forward to it. We were to call at Nagasaki, Kobe and Yokohama and I was determined to see as much of these places as possible. Nagasaki was a great shipbuilding port and we seemed to take ages to negotiate the channel towards the busy harbour. Enormous container ships stood side by side for many miles along the way. We also passed shipbuilding yards where several large super-tankers were being built, including one for P&O.

I was impressed with Japan and the Japanese people. They smiled a lot and although very few spoke English, they were always willing to help out with directions. This caused much hilarity as both sides resorted to mime. In no time a small crowd would gather and with everyone having a different idea of what we were looking for, friendly arguments arose among those trying to help and it sometimes took time to get results. It was all part of the Japanese experience however, and we enjoyed the exchanges. We caused great hilarity when we went into a building we thought was a bank but which turned out to be a garage. We couldn't possibly make that mistake at home.

The temperature in Nagasaki was 90° in the shade, but the humidity was low, so the heat was bearable. Nagasaki was much smaller than I thought it would be; very much like a county town. The houses all had red, blue and orange roofs and were built at the foot of the hills which fringed the town on all sides.

Along with two friends, I took a taxi to the Nagasaki Peace Park commemorating the atomic bombing of Nagasaki on 9th August 1945, which killed 73,000 people and destroyed large parts of the city.

The Peace Park featured a 9.7-metre-high Peace Statue, created to represent the Nagasaki citizens' wish for peace. The right-hand points to the heavens to signify the threat of atomic weapons while the left arm is raised horizontally to represent the wish for peace. The eyes are slightly closed in prayer for the souls of the victims of the bombs. I found the Peace Park a very peaceful and thought-provoking place, but it was nothing to the feelings I had when I entered the War Museum nearby. The museum catalogued the events leading up to the bombing and showed photographs of Nagasaki before and after. The destruction was on a massive scale and the graphic pictures of the injuries inflicted on the people of Nagasaki were horrendous. Walking through the museum was a truly sickening experience.

My companions and I were in need of something pleasant to lift our mood so we visited Glover House, where Puccini lived when he wrote the opera Madame Butterfly. The house was built on a south-facing hill and had a large, lush garden with a wonderful view of the city. A statue of a Japanese geisha girl, supposedly Madame Butterfly of the opera, stood in a secluded spot with a commanding view of the harbour and the sea beyond. It was the perfect place for us to regain our equilibrium after the shock of the museum.

On arrival at Japanese ports, English-speaking Japanese telephonists came aboard and manned the switchboard for the duration of the ship's stay. We reached Kobe at nine o'clock at night, and having settled the Japanese telephonist into her post by the end of my shift at midnight, I joined three female friends for our foray into the world of Japanese sauna culture. Armed with a slip of paper with the name of a sauna, "Kobe Ladies," written in Japanese lettering and another slip saying "Take me please, to SS Orsova berthed in number 5 Imperial Dock" we headed off into the oriental night. A taxi took us to our destination.

The massage parlour was a very up-market affair. A liveried doorman ushered us into a large marble entrance hall, which smelled divine. An efficient receptionist welcomed us (I think), but as she couldn't speak a word of English and we couldn't speak Japanese, we had to rely on mime. This was when the fun really started. We wanted the full works, and after a lot of laughing, waving, pointing and gesticulating, the giggling receptionist got the message. She called for a couple of assistants who handed each of us a large bath sheet, a bar of soap, a toothbrush and toothpaste, and a sachet of shampoo. They pointed towards the changing rooms, then to the lockers, then to a row of open-to-all showers. First of all we stripped and wrapped ourselves in the enormous towels and placed our clothes in one of the lockers before heading for the showers. Not being used to all this open nakedness, we giggled with embarrassment as we attempted to wash our hair, shower and clean our teeth. Mission accomplished, we were ushered, wrapped tightly in our towels, into the sauna which had a temperature of 180° and where we had to stay for seven minutes. The sauna was quite large, circular with three tiers of wooden slatted benches all round. On one wall was a large colour television. None of us had seen colour TV before, so for the first few minutes we were glued to the screen. Then we noticed our companions. There were four or five others there and they were stark naked. Being modest, our towels were still tightly wrapped round us and we were hanging on to them. However, after a few minutes the heat got so bad that we decided to throw caution to the wind and took off the towels.

We were just getting used to our totally naked state, when a girl called us to follow her for the next part of the treatment. Plunging into a cold pool was totally unnerving. Several minutes later and with teeth chattering, we rushed back to the sauna. This pattern was followed three times more. Then it was time for the massage. Not having experienced a massage before, we had no idea what to expect. We were led into a small room where four massage tables stood side by side. What we experienced that night was the ultimate in pain.

I have since discovered that what we experienced that night was Shiatsu, a form of Japanese massage which presses and stimulates the pressure points in the body. It was certainly effective because I was bouncing with energy and couldn't sleep for three nights afterwards.

We could have been forgiven for thinking we'd walked into a club for masochists and sadists. The young masseuses had long bony fingers and they seemed to be picking out the tender spots in our bodies and boring mercilessly into our flesh. The masseuse pulled my toes and kneaded my feet, legs, arms, shoulders, back and neck with fingers of steel. This treatment lasted for about 25 minutes. We were in agony. We yelled, screamed, laughed, squirmed, but nothing eased the pain. The four young masseuses thought our agony was funny and laughed and chatted to each other as we suffered.

Everything comes to an end however, and at last the agony was over. We got dressed and headed for the juice bar where we enjoyed our complimentary glass of blackcurrant juice. But the excitement wasn't over yet.

Out in the bustling city at 4am we tried to find a taxi. There were plenty about. The city was as busy by night as it was by day and the traffic was fast and heavy. Many taxis cruised the streets, but no matter how often we took our lives in our hands dashing into the road to try to attract their attention, we were ignored. We eventually walked to a road junction controlled by traffic lights. "The next taxi that comes along and stops at the lights, we all jump in," someone suggested. It was easier said than done. Taxi drivers shouted at us and tried to drive off, even against the lights. It was frightening. Eventually, we all managed to pile into the taxi of one driver who was taking a message from his controller and unable to shake us off. We showed him the slip of paper with our destination on it and he actually smiled. We got safely home at about six in the morning.

When I related our experiences to one of the Japanese telephonists next day, she said that the massage parlour we had chosen was in the centre of the red light district. Taxi drivers who picked up prostitutes were liable to lose their licence and we were very lucky our driver didn't drive straight to a police station with us. With a straight face she said, "The taxi drivers obviously thought you were prostitutes."

Next day a friend and I went window shopping in the famous Motomache shopping arcade, a mile of covered-in shops selling anything and everything. We had never seen anything like this before. We tried to find a restaurant serving traditional Japanese food, sukiyaki, but very few restaurants in the complex did. "They go in for western type food now," we were told.

Yokohama was our last Japanese port but it was not as nice as Nagasaki and Kobe. Japan had a pollution problem, both in the air and in the sea. There was a permanent haze over Yokohama and I was told that it was even worse in Tokyo. The sea was the dirtiest I had ever seen.

Three of us took the bullet train to Kamakura, half an hour away, where we hired a taxi for three hours to take us round the sights. I had made a list of all the things we wanted to see – The Great Buddha, the Zen Temples, a Japanese Shrine and some Japanese Gardens - and our telephonist/interpreter wrote them out in Japanese. We gave this list to the taxi driver. The Great Buddha didn't disappoint and the Zen Temples took our breath away. We spent some time strolling through a beautiful monastery garden with small tinkling streams crossed by cute little bridges. Lush greenery was abundant and little monkeys played in the trees and came cautiously towards us when we called. We stood at the door of a monastery and listened to the chanting of the Buddhist monks as they said their evening prayers. It was a peaceful interlude. The taxi didn't cost us very much and although the taxi driver couldn't speak any English, we had several hours of very comfortable sightseeing.

We enjoyed ourselves so much in Kamakura that we left if to the last minute to get back to the city for the eight o'clock sailing of the ship that evening. The platform at the railway station was crowded and when a train eventually stopped, there was a mad rush to get on board. We were in danger of being left behind, but we hadn't reckoned on the ingenuity of the Japanese railway guards. They came along the platform and those who were stuck outside the doors of the already bulging train, were pushed, either with hands or a shoulder on the bottom, and squeezed into the compartment. I knew the term "packed like sardines," but this was the first time I'd experienced it.

It was very hot in the crowded carriage and we were gasping for air, so we decided to move up the train to try and find a carriage that wasn't quite so crowded. They were all the same until we reached the first class section, which was empty. We travelled the rest of the journey in comfort until, entering the suburbs of Yokohama, the ticket collector came along. With no common language, we were unable to communicate, but we were perfectly aware that he wanted us to remove ourselves from the carriage. We made a show of getting up and gathering our things when he relented and let us stay.

After an eventful three days in Japan, we sailed that night down the polluted river past the rows of the Japanese Maru company giant tankers lining the long dock side. The sun shone through a yellow screen of pollution. Further down the channel however, it was a lot cleaner and pods of dolphins joined the ship, leaping across the bows and cavorting merrily for several miles while the passengers and crew lined the rails and enjoyed the spectacle. As the sun set, I reflected on a fascinating three days and realised how lucky I was to be enjoying the sights and sounds of foreign countries in a safe and comfortable situation. And there was more to come. Next stop Hawaii.

After leaving Yokohama we ran into a typhoon and everything on board had to be battened down for about eight hours. A large section of casing fell on to one of the decks and it was lucky no-one was underneath. This was also the time that we discovered we had a fire-bug on board. Over a period of five days there were four fires, one of them serious, in the crew quarters. For one of the fires, a bellboy who was unable to sleep alerted the Bridge at half-past-three in the morning.

There were five days at sea before our next port and the crew prepared for the next round of entertainment. Travelling between Yokohama and Honolulu we held a fashion show on consecutive nights in the tourist and first class sections of the ship. Several of the passengers and female members of the crew had had clothes made in Hong Kong and these were shown off at the fashion show. I acted as dresser and it was hard work but enjoyable. After the show we usually retired to someone's cabin and let our hair down. It was disappointing just to have one day in Honolulu, especially when there was so much to do there. I went for a swim at Waikiki in the morning but had to be back on board by 12.30 for my switch-board duties. In the evening I went for a meal to the Waikiki Tower Revolving Restaurant with six others. The views of Honolulu were superb, and we had a great feast and got merry on Mai-tais. We just made it back to the ship in time for our midnight sailing.

After our one-day visit to Honolulu we had another four days at sea and this time we held an Olde Tyme Music Hall. I was wardrobe mistress and make-up artist. It too, was hard work. After the show the cast retired to the Tourist Playroom where the Staff Captain had arranged a fantastic buffet. We relaxed with a sing-song afterwards. Next day we discovered that nine cases of beer had been drunk during the music hall and quite a few bottles of wine with the food afterwards, so there would have been a few sore heads next day. At the music hall in the first class section the following night, the beer was rationed. We all retired to the playroom again for food and drink, but I could see that everyone was set for another wild night and I left, knowing my constitution couldn't cope with two hectic nights in a row.

Our visit to Los Angeles was a short one of just ten hours and I worked most of this time to allow Rita to have the day off. As we left Los Angeles, a group of us sat down to mince and tatties, cooked by Alison. She enjoyed cooking and often made stovies or mince and tatties, good Scots staples. She also went on food-buying sprees at some of the ports.

We arrived at San Francisco at three o'clock the following afternoon and Alison, Mona and I were off immediately for a visit to Cost+, a well-known American supermarket where we stocked up on food and wine. I had never seen a supermarket as big as this. That night we enjoyed bread and butter, salami, cheese and pickles in Alison's cabin with a few friends and finished off the night having a party and a sing-song in the cabin of one of the engineers.

Next morning I was up early for a six-to-nine morning shift, after which I went shopping with Claire the "disco-dolly." I was buying a dress and shoes for wearing out to dinner that evening. Lunch of seafood followed at Fisherman's Wharf where we were joined by two of the ship's officers who gallantly paid for the lunch. After working until half past seven that evening, it was on with the glad-rags and off to a very plush restaurant called the Blue Fox.

As we sat in the bar, the barman chatted. "I had a fellow Englishman in earlier" he ventured. "Lord Furness. Do you know him?" I took a fit of the giggles. No wonder. He was only the Chairman of P&O! After a fantastic dinner, which I couldn't appreciate fully as I'd eaten too much at lunchtime, we finished off our evening with a visit to the disco at the Top of the Fairmont Hotel, supposed to be the "in" place in San Francisco and the place to spot celebrities. It obviously wasn't the night for celebs and after a short visit to the jazz club in the basement of the hotel, we headed back to the ship for a fairly early night.

I always enjoyed getting up early in port and next morning I

Old Tyme Music Hall.

was up at the crack of dawn when I walked along to Fisherman's Wharf. The stall holders were just setting up for the day and they and the squawking gulls were my only company. I always approached each port as if it was my one and only visit there and I might not return, so I tried hard to implant the impression of the place firmly on my memory and describe it later in my diary. I fell in with Allan, who had the same idea as me, for a quiet stroll. We sat on the pier drinking in the atmosphere, and enjoyed a coffee at an open-air café before wandering back to the ship for my stint on duty at half-past-eight. We sailed at one o'clock.

Vancouver was a non-day for me as I worked extra hours paying back one of the telephonists. There followed four days at sea and the entertainment this time was Casino Night where I manned the roll-the-penny stall with Mona. The passengers weren't exactly spendthrift and our takings amounted to £26 in the first class and £17 in the tourist class two nights later.

Honolulu was the next stop and off I went to Waikiki Beach, my very favourite spot. To swim in the warm gentle water was heaven. Ross, the hospital attendant came with me and we decided that this was the day we were going to try surfing. Waikiki has about five or six days a year when there is no surf and unfortunately this was one of them. There was plenty to do however, and swimming and shopping, eating and drinking featured highly that day. As we sat on the sand at Waikiki drinking our Blue Hawaiians, we watched the most glorious sunset. The sun, all golden, orange and red and mirroring these colours on the smooth water, sank slowly into the sea. As soon as the great red ball disappeared over the horizon, everything went black. Night comes suddenly in Hawaii.

On the journey between Hawaii and Fiji, our next entertainment evening was Island Night and a group of eight girls began rehearsals for our party piece: a hula dance. Noreen, the hostess, was the organiser of this and on our last visit to Suva we'd bought hula skirts and leis. The music was bought in Hawaii and we were all ready to get the rehearsals under way. We met in one of the playrooms. Our first performance in the First Class section of the ship was a great success. Prior to the performance, we'd been treated to a couple of bottles of champagne by the Staff Captain so we were in a relaxed mood for the evening ahead. When our turn came we carried off our performance with great panache and revelled in the loud applause that followed and seemed to go on and on. Our second performance in the Tourist section of the ship was no less successful and when it was over we retired to one of the public rooms to enjoy yet another celebratory drink and buffet.

On our next visit to Suva, I was met by Frances and Dan Marshall from Inverness and taken to their home for the evening. Dan worked as a telephone engineer in Inverness and Frances and I worked together in the Inverness Telephone Exchange in the 1950s. Dan was on a two-year deployment helping the Fiji Government bring their telephone system up to date. They loved Fiji and were making the most of their stay there. Their two children were quite small but they would have to return home after their two-year stint for schooling. I think they would have liked to stay in Fiji a bit longer, but it wasn't to be.

I was never short of company on *Orsova*. Bernie was the Second Steward and I couldn't stand him. He had a loud voice, was bossy and very rude. We had a couple of run-ins when he refused to let myself and Ros off the ship until all the passengers had gone ashore. I got wise to Bernie however, and usually managed to slip ashore when he wasn't looking.

Bernie began inviting me to his cabin for a meal and a drink and initially I refused. He wasn't my favourite person and I had no inclination to spend an evening in his company when there was so much else I could be doing. He persisted, however, so I thought I'd go just the once to get rid of him. What a surprise I got. The transformation in the man was amazing. He was the perfect gentleman. It turned out he was very knowledgeable about classical music and for the rest of the voyage I paid several visits to his cabin for drinks, a meal and a musical evening. My knowledge of classical music was practically non-existent, although I was fond of it, so Bernie set about teaching me. He would play one or two pieces each time and would tell me all about the composer, when it was composed and why. He then went on to describe each movement and what instruments were being played. My musical education was greatly advanced by my visits to Bernie. Our relationship was comfortable, purely platonic and one that I enjoyed. I still didn't get priority disembarking!

When the ship next arrived in Sydney, Ann Jack, an old school friend from Avoch, was waiting on the quay with her two children. Ann and her husband Don had migrated to Australia after their marriage in the early sixties. They took me to their home for the afternoon where we caught up with all the news of Avoch and the Black Isle. This was the first time Ann and Don had met someone from home since they settled in Australia, so we had plenty to talk about. When I returned to the ship in the late afternoon, Ann and family came on board and had a good look round. The children especially, enjoyed the visit.

We now had three days in Sydney and according to my diary my evenings were spent enjoying the good things in life such as theatre trips, fine dining and champagne. I embraced it all, but my constitution wasn't as strong as those who had been to sea for years and I suffered badly. After three days I was glad to set sail out of Sydney.

I obviously hadn't learned my lesson from our last stay in

Sydney, that wining and dining too regularly didn't agree with me, and I note from my diary that I did exactly the same thing in Melbourne. Four of us went for lunch to an Italian restaurant called Florentinos, where we ate too much, drank too much and had to return to the ship early as none of us was in any fit state to do any sightseeing. In Adelaide, our next stop, I chose my company carefully and went ashore with Maggie Pile where we strolled along the wide tree-lined streets so clean and green, and drank nothing stronger than milk shakes.

Crossing the Australian Bight was horrendous: high winds, rain and heavy seas meant that the ship tossed about a lot and many of the passengers were sick. The dining room most evenings was empty. It was a relief to reach Fremantle two days later.

My second visit to Perth was about as exciting as the first and I note in my diary that I went on a tour but I don't say where to. I ended the trip in the city centre traipsing round the shops with someone called Bobbi and I wasn't happy. It was a relief to get back to the ship for my next turn on duty at four o'clock that afternoon. I enjoyed sausage, bacon and eggs in someone's cabin that night and it was the highlight of my day!

Our eight days' voyage across the Indian Ocean was uneventful. When we weren't entertaining the passengers with the various themed nights, we were catching up on our sleep. I mention in my diary that the cabin I shared with Ros was becoming like a home for lonely sailors as Bob and Harold were regular callers, usually carrying a bottle of whisky which they drank between them, not leaving until it was empty. Ros and I stuck to sherry or coffee, as we hadn't the stamina to keep up with Bob and Harold. I must have been very tolerant of these lovable drunks, which is what they were, because I can't see me being so sympathetic nowadays towards a couple of drunks, no matter how lovable.

When I went ashore in Durban I experienced a feeling of tension which I hadn't encountered on my last visit. There was an atmosphere in the Indian market and the stallholders weren't all that friendly, so we cut our visit short and headed for the beach. In the evening I was supposed to be heading ashore for another night of fine dining, but my date "forgot" and spent the evening on board at an all-male "do". I wasn't too pleased, but Alison came to the

Bernie Edwards and nursing sister. Photo: Seadogs Reunited

rescue and provided steak rolls and rum punch for a few friends in her cabin.

Orsova docked at Port Elizabeth at eight o'clock in the morning and I was off the ship soon after as I had to be on duty again at one o'clock that afternoon. I was accompanied by Ross, the hospital attendant, who was as keen as I was to see something of the city.

Our first stop was the Campanile Tower at the entrance to the railway station directly opposite the harbour. The Campanile (meaning Bell Tower in Italian) was built in 1920 to mark the centenary of the arrival in 1820 of British settlers who came to populate the hinterland of the Eastern Cape.

We climbed 204 steps to the observation room where the 360° view of the harbour and surrounding area was magnificent. After enjoying the sight of our ship lying in the harbour and after trying, not very successfully, to locate various places mentioned in our Port Notes, we headed for the George IV Park. It was very quiet with not many people about. The Orchid House was impressive and for some reason, I picked an orchid. Ross was a bit embarrassed and kept looking around in case someone had noticed and was about to throw us out. What with the all-pervading CCTV of today, I wouldn't get away with it now, but I wasn't rumbled this time. We lingered for a time in the park where we had a picnic, then had to make a dash back to the ship in time for my stint on duty at one o'clock.

Next day we arrived in Cape Town at four o'clock in the afternoon. I expected to be out on the town wining and dining, but I'd been "stood up" yet again by my friend. Never happy to spend time on board if we can get ashore, Alison, Noreen, Maggie P and I went to the Harbour Café, a pretty rough establishment, but serving excellent food. I soon eased myself into the swing of the evening and drowned my sorrows in fine style, ably accompanied by my three companions.

Sharing a cabin with someone is not ideal, especially when you don't feel too well. I had occasion to visit the surgery for treatment for a sore throat and spent my off-duty time that afternoon in bed. I worked from 7.30 to midnight and was looking forward to falling into my bed with a hot toddy at the end of my shift, but when I got to the cabin, Ros, Harold and another crew member were having a drinking session and all three were completely stoned. It was Ros's birthday. Having a sensible conversation with them was impossible, so I went off to the galley and made myself a hot toddy there. By the time I returned at about one o'clock, I met Ros and her friends in the corridor, reeling away to another venue to continue their binge.

Tenerife, the largest of seven inhabited islands which form the Canary Archipelago, was our next destination. For such a small island, it packs a wealth of history. The capital, Santa Cruz, where we were berthed, was founded by Alvaro Fernandez de Lugo, who conquered the island in 1496.

On 25th July 1797, Rear-Admiral Horatio Nelson led an attack on the capital. He was repulsed, but lost his right arm in the conflict. In 1936 Tenerife also made an important contribution to Spanish history when Generalissimo Franco, then Captain-General of the Canaries, gathered together the officers of the garrison of Tenerife for the National Rising, which started the Spanish Civil War.

I joined a tour across the island to La Laguna, six-and-a-half miles from the capital and nestling in the valley of Aguere at the gateway to the Anaga Mountains. La Laguna is the oldest city on the island and according to my port notes, the most interesting. It was the capital of Tenerife until 1921 when Santa Cruz took over. The tomb of Alvaro Fernandes de Lugo, the founder of Santa Cruz and the conqueror of Tenerife, lies in the cathedral. La Laguna also boasts a university which was founded in 1701.

A few weeks later, we had another short stop at Tenerife when six of us hired a taxi to Mount Teide, an active volcano which rises to over 12,000 feet. Tenerife has no winter due to the Gulf Stream, and the summers are never excessively hot because of the constant breezes which blow from the north-east. Owing to the great differences in altitude in such a small area, it is possible to participate in winter sports on Mount Teide, while only twelve miles away others are enjoying swimming and sun-bathing on the coast. We found most of the island to be covered in volcanic rock, and the sand on the beaches, black. It was a clear day when we climbed Mount Teide. The taxi only took us part of the way and we had a stiff climb to the summit. The view from the top was worth the effort however, where the island spread out before us into the distance.

Our penultimate port on this trip was Lisbon and I went ashore with Maggie Farmer for a busy day of sightseeing. We took a taxi to the Statue of Christ where we climbed to the top to enjoy the wonderful views of the city and the surrounding countryside. The Mosteiro dos Jerónimos with its magnificent church, was next on our list.

According to my Port Notes, the Mosteiro dos Jerónimos, was historically associated with the early explorers, and it was here that Vasco da Gama spent his last night before his voyage to explore the far-east. The church attached to the monastery was constructed on his return, to commemorate his discovery of the sea route to India. The church is famed for its magnificent cloisters and columns, each one with different carvings of coils of rope, sea monsters, coral and other sea motifs evocative of that time of world exploration.

We then took the train to Cascais, a small fishing port twenty miles away, which during the second world war, increased its population by about twenty-thousand due to the influx of several European Heads of State and Royalty who, together with other aristocrats, politicians, actors, writers and spies, sought refuge from the war.

In the evening I was wined and dined at one of Lisbon's many superb restaurants. This one was "all plush and chandeliers" according to my diary and we dined royally on steak and champagne.

After a calm transit of the Bay of Biscay, we arrived at our last port on this round trip, Rotterdam, where Maggie P and I went ashore with £4 between us. We bought tulip bulbs and nick-nacks and even managed a cup of coffee, so the pound must have been pretty strong in 1972. After dinner that night I was invited to a farewell champagne party to celebrate the departure of Alison and the Chief Officer. It was a riotous affair where we sang naughty songs well into the early hours.

Tuesday, 17th October, arrival day at Southampton. I didn't have to work so was able to have an extra hour or two in bed before passing through customs and pay-off. Customs charged me £12 duty for my Hong Kong pearls, two pounds more than I paid for them. I headed off up to Bristol for the night to enjoy a soft bed that didn't move and the best sleep I'd had for a few weeks.

Part 7

Cruising

West Indies, West Africa and Madeira
October 1972 to November 1972

Sailing day was Friday 20th October. It was cold, and with embar-kation in full swing, all the doors were open and a fierce draught was sweeping its way along the corridors. For once I didn't go on deck to see us sail.

It poured rain all the way to Madeira, and even there it was cold and wet, the first time we'd had bad weather there. I went ashore with a group to the A-Seta restaurant, our regular destination when in Funchal. We sat on wooden benches and ate chicken with our fingers while drinking in the magnificent view from the terrace.

When we arrived in Antigua, five of us hired a taxi for a trip to Nelson's Dockyard, a very old, very British dockyard situated on the south coast of Antigua in the narrow bay of English Harbour. According to my ever-faithful port notes, it was built in the eigh-teenth century, reportedly with slave labour, and designed to deal with the constant struggle between the navies of Britain and France as they vied for superiority in the Atlantic Ocean.

The dockyard was given its name because Nelson was based there between 1784 and 1787. His job was to enforce British rules on trade with the newly-founded United States of America, and his harassment of merchants made him an unpopular figure. In letters and writings, Nelson describes the dockyard as an "insufferable hole" and a "vile spot" where he was "most woefully pinched" by mosquitoes. I think we can assume that he didn't much care for his temporary home. The inhabitants didn't exactly care for Nelson either, and his promotion and departure appear to have been mourned by few.

After an exhausting tour of the dockyard, we found the most wonderful beach which looked as if it had come straight out of a tourist brochure: a long stretch of silver sand fringed with palm trees and water whose colour defied description. We enjoyed a late picnic lunch, lay on the beach and had a swim before heading back to the ship and boarding in the nick of time for sailing.

We woke up next day to the news that there was an enteric epidemic on board and many of the passengers and crew were sick and confined to their cabins. For the next six days, as we crossed the Atlantic, the medical staff worked non-stop to try to contain the spread of this infectious illness. By the time we reached Vigo it was all over. Rough weather was expected in the Bay of Biscay, and true to form the passengers all took to their beds again for the day-long transit.

Our two-day turnaround in Southampton was exceptionally busy and I seemed to be working most of the time. It was a relief to set sail. Agadir, in Morocco was our first stop. This was a port I hadn't visited before so I was looking forward to a few hours of sightseeing and had arranged to go ashore with three friends when my shift ended at 12.30.

Agadir is located on the fringe of a bay of golden sand more than five miles long. To the north the Atlas Mountains tumble into the sea, with their last outpost, the Hill of Anza, overlooking Agadir from a height of 750 feet. Perched on top of the hill are the ruins of an old fortress or kasbah, but in 1972 only the ramparts were left intact, sole testimony to Agadir's earlier history.

Agadir in 1972 was still a fairly small town. It was laid waste by an earthquake in 1960, when fifteen thousand of its inhabitants, one third of the population at the time, were killed. It was quick to recover, and work on its redevelopment began almost immediately. The port and industrial quarters were the first to be rebuilt, followed by the tourist and holiday areas. According to my port notes, Agadir was now a model of town planning and expansion, with wide avenues, large buildings and comfortable villas surrounded by gardens. Several hotels had been built along the seafront and the town had recently been accorded the title, "The Nice of Morocco."

Together with Allan, Maggie Farmer and Noreen, we hired a taxi for four hours and asked the driver to take us into the desert to a place where there were no tourists. We drove along desert tracks to a village about twenty miles east of the town. On the way we saw, not far away, a camel train of about ten or twelve camels driven by men in vivid blue robes. Our guide informed us they were Berbers.

Berbers are believed to have populated Morocco for almost five thousand years. They were made up of various tribes who originally migrated from Libya and Ethiopia and were collectively known as Berbers. Originally pagan worshippers, they now appear to have embraced Islam, Christianity and Judaism.

We came to a fairly substantial village which had a large market selling fruit and vegetables, clothes, pots and pans and other sundries. There was not another tourist in sight. Our taxi driver was a mine of information. He explained the different races, religions, the various languages used and some of the history of the area. He acted as guide and interpreter when we wanted to speak to the stall holders who were a bit shy and avoided our gaze. When one of our group tried to take photographs, they looked away. We were a tourist attraction to them however, as this was not a place that the ship's passengers visited. We noticed that when they thought we weren't looking, they studied us intently. Maggie and I bought kaftans, elegant gowns which we wore a lot on board.

In the village square, we came upon an old man sitting beside a barrel of fresh dates. The top of the barrel had a thick layer of flies on it and a cloud of the blighters was flying around the top of the barrel waiting for an opportunity to land. The man himself was filthy. His hands were ingrained with dirt and he looked as if he hadn't seen soap and water for many years, far less weeks or days. He picked up a date from the top of the barrel and proffered it to me. Horrified, but not wanting to offend the man, I looked towards

Allan. "Take it," he advised. "If you get ill I've got plenty medicines to cure you." I said I would accept the date only if the others did so too. So we all accepted a lovely fresh date from the dirty hands of the old man and covered in germs from the multitude of flies, and none of us got sick.

Our next stop was to a café in the village where our taxi driver treated us all to mint tea and small sweet cakes. The taxi driver certainly earned his fare that day, together with a big fat tip for his kindness. We then bought a large bag of juicy oranges before heading back to the ship.

Next day I was invited to a drinks party where the head barman had created a cocktail in the colours of the P&O flag, with curry powder to represent India, and decorated with an axe to celebrate the P&O shareholders' rejection of the Bovis bid for the company. I hadn't a clue what it was all about but I celebrated nevertheless. The cocktail itself was pretty forgettable.

I woke next morning to find that the ship was moving very slowly. The engines were labouring and the vibration of the ship was particularly bad. There was a problem with one of the engines, but it couldn't have been that bad because the Chief Engineer, a Scotsman, was entertaining passengers and senior officers (and me) at midday, and he didn't appear to have a care in the world as he poured out liberal quantities of his best malt whisky. Fortunately, the engineers were all busy below decks and had the faulty engine up and running after a few hours.

Lisbon was the last port before many of the crew were leaving and there was a party atmosphere on board. I was supposed to be going out that evening in a group of eight, but some had celebrated too much earlier in the day and weren't up to socialising. One or two were suffering from a sickness bug that had taken hold among the passengers and crew a few days before, so the party was reduced to two. My friend was leaving the ship in Southampton so this was to be a special occasion. The evening started so well. A bottle of the best champagne was demolished before we even left the ship.

The city centre restaurant we went to was grand and the food even grander. I had an aperitif, a dry martini, straight gin and vermouth and very strong! We shared a bottle of red wine with the meal. Moving on to a nightclub, we devoured another bottle of champagne while we watched a programme of Fado, the mournful music of Portugal. On the way back to the ship I began to find it difficult to get my legs to do what I wanted them to do and I got back to my cabin in the nick of time.

That night, sailing from Lisbon was an occasion that many of the crew on board would remember, or not, as the case may be. Nowadays drinking among the officers, especially the senior officers, is not tolerated, but in 1972 it wasn't seen as a problem. It was rumoured that as we sailed out of Lisbon that night, the only sober person on the Bridge was the Junior Third Officer. I hope it was just a rumour. We arrived safely in Southampton a few days later and with three weeks before *Orsova* embarked on a Christmas Cruise, followed by another round the world trip, I headed for Rosemarkie.

Part 8

A Cruise to Forget

The Christmas Cruise, 1972

The 1972 Christmas Cruise was one I think many of the crew would prefer to forget. During three weeks in port, Southampton Health officials, in their efforts to trace the dysentery bug that had plagued the previous two cruises, tried to undertake medical tests, but the regular European crew had all departed on leave and the only people left on board were the Goanese. They complained that they were being discriminated against. When they refused to take the tests, 212 Goanese crewmen were dismissed.

The problem hadn't been resolved by sailing day. On 17th December I noted in my diary: "Can't get away from Southampton quickly enough. I think this is going to be a disastrous cruise." *Orsova* sailed with only 600 of the original 1,100 passengers booked, the remaining passengers having been offered an alternative cruise. The all-white replacement crew, which I describe in my diary as "the roughest, toughest, dirtiest-looking lot I've ever seen," included forty boys who were half-way through a catering course at the local technical college and who had never set foot on a ship before. They were all sea-sick by the second day out.

Complaints from the passengers started even before we left the quay and they continued until the cruise ended on 2nd January. The girls in the telephone exchange were frequently the first contact for complaints and the passengers were not slow to let their

104

feelings be known, usually in the rudest way possible. It was difficult to keep calm at times.

Some of the passengers formed a committee with the express purpose of getting their money back, so they complained about anything and everything, no matter how trivial. To make matters worse, our first port of call was to be Agadir, but the weather was too rough to land and we anchored offshore for several hours hoping for a change in the weather. It was decided eventually to sail for Las Palmas, the next port on our itinerary. I noted in my diary "the weather is improving but the passengers' tempers are not".

As if it wasn't bad enough having to deal with disgruntled passengers, during our overnight stay in Las Palmas we had to contend with an unruly crew. Most of them headed for the town bars where they drank to excess and stocked up on Bacardi, which was cheap. According to my diary, "they were hardly sober until Boxing Day."

We had just begun a new shift system in the telephone exchange, where we worked four days on each shift, and it was just my luck that on the four days in the run-up to Christmas Day, I was on night shift. My time was spent each night contacting the doctors to attend to the many injuries, some being cuts with bottles, caused by fights among the crew. Knowing that they were only temporary employees and would be out of a job at the end of the cruise, made these men fearless, and discipline was not something they recognised.

There was, for me, a rather sad incident during our cruise. One of the young students, a boy of fifteen, was assigned to the Telephone Exchange as a bellboy. He'd never been to sea before, and this would be the first time he was away from home for Christmas, so I took an interest in him and got to know him quite well. He told me about his family and about his girlfriend. He was a good worker and carried out his duties delivering messages between cabins, the Bureau, the Bridge and the telephone exchange, in an efficient way and we got on well. When it was quiet we played scrabble and draughts.

When I was ashore in Las Palmas I was horrified to see our bellboy out on the town with a group of homosexual waiters who were making their noisy way into a bar. For a start our bellboy was too young to be drinking and secondly I knew that there were one or two predatory homosexuals in the group and I feared for the boy's safety.

On my next shift, I wondered why the bellboy hadn't turned up for duty, and when I made enquiries, I discovered that he had taken up a post outside the telephone exchange and was taking messages from me by telephone only. I was mystified. I couldn't think of anything I'd done to offend him. All was revealed however, when he eventually had to come to the exchange with a message and I discovered that he had a huge bruise, a "love bite," on his neck. I could only assume that he had been targeted by one of the homosexuals who, having plied him with alcohol, then sexually assaulted him. For the rest of the cruise he kept well away from the telephone exchange except when he had to take or deliver a message and not once did he meet my eye or speak to me other than to pass on messages.

To my eternal shame, I did nothing about it and many years later when I told Derek Hansing, who was the Captain of *Orsova* at the time, about the incident, he went into a terrible rage and gave me a proper dressing-down. The boy was underage and the Captain was responsible for the welfare of these vulnerable crew members. The person who carried out the assault on the boy would have been thrown in jail, I was told, and would have been handed over to the police on our return to Southampton. Being an ex-policewoman who had dealt with assaults, sexual and otherwise, I should have known this and I certainly was guilty of dereliction of duty that day. This incident is something that I often recall with sadness that I failed to protect a vulnerable boy by turning a blind eye to a possible crime.

In spite of all the trouble on board, the officers and crew were determined that Christmas would be celebrated, and the parties and pour-outs continued. I joined the crew choir and went carol singing through the public rooms on Christmas Eve. We ended our tour of the ship in the crew rec room, but the crew were all pretty drunk and they weren't interested in listening to our crooning, so we cut our visit short and went back to the public rooms for an encore. I had to work a night shift from midnight, so I had to refrain from celebrating further.

On Christmas Day I had three hours sleep, then Ros and I opened our presents together. It was a busy day of partying and the first pour-out was in the Chief Radio Officer's cabin at eleven-thirty, followed by drinks with the Captain at noon. A superb Christmas Dinner in the Tourist Restaurant followed, and Ros and I were given permission to invite Bob the Plumber to join us. Waiter service didn't extend to the telephonists and stewardesses due to the lack of waiting staff, so we had to collect our food from the galley.

The last time I spent Hogmanay at sea was when I was part-way through my first voyage on Iberia somewhere in the southern hemisphere, and it was bit of a non-event. This time we were in the Atlantic between Madeira and Southampton and I decided that I was going to have a party to celebrate. I was working until eight-thirty that evening, but all I had to do was get dressed as Bob and Harold had arranged everything, even the food. They set up a bar in the next-door cabin which was occupied by the ship's musicians, but as they were to be working late, they had no objections to their cabin being used. I just had to sit back and wait for the guests to arrive. We had no idea who would come as Ros and I had issued an open invitation to all and sundry, so I was pleased when the Captain and his First Officer, plus several of the deck officers arrived and helped out with the singing of a few Scots songs.

At two minutes to midnight Ros arrived, followed – at a brisk trot – by several of the Bureau staff, and we all filled our glasses and sang Auld Lang Syne. We were three hours into the New Year before the last reveller departed and Ros and I had to clear up, as 1st January was peak day and the inspecting officer would not have appreciated a messy cabin, even if he had been at the party the night before. I had a few hours' sleep before my shift at nine o'clock, and after that it was off on the round of New Year's Day parties. I'm afraid I was a bit shattered and had to turn down several invitations and have an early night.

When we reached Southampton on 2nd January, a surprise was in store: our next sailing was a whole week away on Tuesday the ninth. I had gone back to bed after my shift and didn't find out until two that afternoon, so there was a mad rush to get myself home to Rosemarkie. I managed to get on a train to London, then

107

on to the night sleeper to Inverness. There were no berths available, but at least I had a seat. The train was packed to capacity with many sitting in the corridor, and some of the passengers were drunk, but I managed to get some sleep.

It was good to get home for the four days. News travels fast and my mother knew all about the horrendous time we'd had on the Christmas cruise. It was front page news in several newspapers and she had collected them all to show me. The passengers, in their fight for compensation, had made sure the country was informed about the deprivation and discomfort they had experienced. Unfortunately, a lot of what was written I recognised, but things had settled down and for most of the cruise, it was fairly quiet. It all blew over soon enough with the passengers accepting full compensation.

I had to leave on the Saturday evening to catch the London sleeper. Once again there were no berths available and I had a long uncomfortable night ahead of me, but I took one of my mother's sleeping pills and had a reasonable night.

Part 9

Round the World 3

*Southampton to Sydney via the Panama Canal
and Sydney to Southampton via the Cape
January 1973 to April 1973*

I should have been on board *Orsova* at ten o'clock in the morning, but the train was late getting into London and it was two o'clock before I arrived. Next morning we had boat drill, and because Rita was ill, I had to man the switchboard for her. I had a shock when our new captain and the inspecting party came to the telephone exchange to see why I wasn't at my boat station. I didn't know whether to be pleased or annoyed. At these crew stations, one was liable to be asked questions about evacuation or fire safety, or any element of procedure involving your boat station. I'd never been asked a question before, but when the captain posed a question, and I was able to answer it, he went away looking slightly bemused.

We were now sailing with a full Indian crew, but we still had a few problems. They had been recruited in Calcutta and many of them had never been on a British ship before. I wrote to my mother: "They're all old and they don't understand English very well, so the menus have to be numbered. One day the nursing sister asked for number nine, which was soufflé, and back came the waiter with nine soufflés."

The passengers on this trip were a pleasant lot and they all set off on their various tours in cheerful mood. It was so much easier for the crew if they were happy. Four hundred and four passengers were doing the round trip and we had on board Jean Plaidy, the author, who held weekly book-signing sessions.

Our first port of call was Madeira. My friends and I found ourselves in a warehouse where we were shown a huge number of baskets ready for exporting to America. The obligatory tour of a winery was next, and once again we got the full works from one of the guides, taking us through the process of blending, bottling, labelling and storing. Sampling from several of the vats was also included in the tour. We then stocked up for the voyage ahead.

When we entered the Atlantic proper, the weather turned cold and the sea rough. Many of the passengers were seasick, but they were no bother at all and just took to their beds to ride out the storm without complaint. I wished all passengers were like them. We had a couple of days when there was a huge swell with the ship pitching and tossing and rolling from side to side, but the captain refused to extend the stabilisers as they slowed the ship down and used up more fuel.

Hamilton, Bermuda was our first stop across the Atlantic. I went ashore on the first tender, straight off night shift. Six of us hired mopeds. I had Noreen as my passenger and we changed places half way. No licence required! I'd never driven a moped before but after a few wobbles I soon got into the swing of things and we tootled round the island, first to the west and then to the east. The speed limit was fifteen miles an hour, but we didn't find this out until much later. We had coffee in Somerset at the west of the island and then set about finding a picnic place, which was not difficult as Bermuda's beautiful sandy beaches stretched right round the island. Not wanting to return to the ship too early, we sat on the quay in the warm sunshine and caught the last tender back to the ship. I managed a couple of hours sleep before going on duty at nine that night. I was very tired, very sore and glad to be on the move again.

Port Everglades was our next stop. We arrived late afternoon, but the immigration authorities took so long to clear the crew that it was too late for me to go ashore as I was on duty at midnight. I

Miami from the top of the Fontainbleu Hotel.

mention in my diary that I went on deck prior to going on night shift and it was a wonderful evening: a full moon shone on a calm sea and a gentle breeze tangled with the palm trees, allowing them to sway gracefully to and fro. Next day we had an early boat drill and my boat was lowered for a short run round the harbour.

After boat drill I went into Miami with Noreen, Allan, Carol and two photographers. Noreen hired a car, a huge beast the size of a small bus, and we drove through the streets of Miami just looking at the imposing buildings. The road junctions and flyovers were puzzles the like of which we'd never seen before, but Noreen did a sterling job. We headed for Miami Beach and passed rows of towering hotels and huge mansions. We decided to enter the Fontainbleu Hotel, the most luxurious on Collins Avenue in Millionaires Row, Miami, "just for a look" and when no-one challenged us, we took the lift up to the top floor where the view of Miami was magnificent. A drink in the bar was suggested, but one look at the prices and we decided not to bother.

Sailing out of Port Everglades that evening was quite an experience. Many of the residents of the flats by the entrance to the harbour had put all their lights on and were standing on their balconies waving flags and sounding klaxons as we glided past.

111

Nassau was our next stop. According to my Port Notes, Nassau, in New Providence Island, is the capital of the Bahamas, an archipelago of the British West Indies consisting of more than 3,000 islands, cays and rocks extending from Florida to Haiti, a distance of about 760 miles. Only 22 of the islands are inhabited. The Bahamas ensured their place in history when Christopher Columbus, under Spanish patronage, landed at San Salvador, a small island on the outward fringe of the archipelago, on 12th October 1492 on his first voyage of discovery. The Spanish had failed to colonise the island, however, and in 1627 British settlement began.

During the latter part of the seventeenth century, the settlement suffered frequent depredations by the Spanish and French and became a favourite rendezvous of pirates. A fort was built in 1695 to protect the inhabitants of the city, formerly named Charles Towne but renamed Nassau. After Britain abolished the international slave trade in 1807, thousands of Africans liberated from slave ships by the Royal Navy, were resettled on New Providence Island and on several of the other Caribbean islands. At the beginning of the twentieth century, sea communications between the Islands and America were improved, and a great tourist industry was born.

We reached our berth at eight o'clock in the morning. I went for a walk along the quay where small boats loaded with conch shells, bananas, pigs and goats, chickens, vegetables, fruit and fish, sailed in and tied up alongside the quay. In no time a market was in full swing.

Once again Noreen hired a car, and a group of us drove all round the island. There was a distinct division of cultures: one side of the island was spectacular with lovely beaches, palm trees and huge villas, the Bahamas being rated as a millionaires' playground; the other side was decidedly scruffy with small shanty towns with dusty streets and packs of children and dogs everywhere. We didn't tarry long there. In the late afternoon, I watched from the deck of Orsova, five other cruise ships sail just before us.

Montego Bay, Jamaica was superb: a turquoise sea shone like a mirror, reflecting a multitude of yachts sporting many-coloured sails. Once again we anchored in the bay and were taken ashore by tender. From the ship, the island looked very green and lush with bursts of purple bougainvillea and sparkling white buildings peeping through. Along with Allan, Maggie F, Mona and Noreen, we hired a taxi for a couple of hours and drove through the town, past the airport where we saw many beautiful luxury homes dotted around. We also drove through fields of sugar cane, still the biggest export in Jamaica. Our taxi driver was a bit surly and told us that the British were not well liked on the island. When we alighted to take a look around, the people were not at all friendly and we didn't see a smiling face all afternoon. I have recently been researching the Jamaican slave trade and Britain's role in it, and I'm not surprised they don't like us much, although I would have thought that a few generations forward they would have forgiven us by now.

Christopher Columbus first explored Jamaica in 1494 when the island was inhabited by Arawak Indians who had migrated from South America. Spanish settlers arrived in 1510 to raise cattle and pigs. They were the first to import African slaves to Jamaica to work in the sugar fields. By the end of the sixteenth century the Arawak population had been wiped out by hard labour and ill treatment by the Spanish and European diseases to which they had no resistance. When the island was invaded by the British in 1655, the Spanish, having failed to find gold and other precious metals on the island, surrendered or fled to Cuba.

British settlers were encouraged to settle on the island and the British Government introduced several Acts of Parliament granting them parcels of land. There began a proliferation of plantations growing sugar and other crops such as tobacco, indigo and cocoa, all of which were transported across the Atlantic to British ports. The profits from the plantations were ploughed into houses and businesses, as well as public buildings.

In my diary I mention that I stood on deck for a long time that night just looking at the stars, which were brilliant. It was a warm night and the ship was cruising slowly towards our next port of call. Just before midnight we arrived at Cristobal on the eastern side of the Panama Canal, where dozens of ships were queuing to transit at first light. No shore leave was allowed as we were due to begin our transit at six in the morning.

As we glided slowly westwards through the canal that day, the twenty-fifth of January, we celebrated the birth of Scotland's national poet Rabbie Burns with a drinks party at lunchtime in my cabin. I had my trusty poetry book with me and we had a giggle hearing Tam O'Shanter read in Scots, English, Welsh, Irish and Australian. In the evening Mona arranged a Burns Supper of haggis, neeps and tatties washed down with whisky. The chef on *Orsova* was a Scot and he always carried a plentiful supply of tinned haggis.

Orsova was spending eighteen hours in Acapulco and I had twelve hours off. A group of six arranged to go ashore to sample the local food, drink and customs. Not for us the touristy restaurants of the water front, blaring pop music and serving steak and chips and warm beer, but the more sophisticated back street eating places frequented by the locals and serving only authentic dishes. Perhaps we might be lucky enough to find some Mexican entertainment.

It was a lovely evening as we stepped on to the ship's launch for the short journey ashore. The sea was calm, the air warm and the lights of the town inviting. We strolled past the crowded restaurants and shops and made our way to the lesser known quarter of the town. Some children stared at us shyly then ran away giggling and chattering to each other.

Soon we came to a narrow street which sported several restaurants: all small, dimly lit and housing only a handful of local residents. We chose a restaurant which was clean and not too crowded. The menu, displayed prominently at the entrance, promised interesting food at a price we could afford.

The proprietor, a small fat man with a thin droopy moustache, greeted us warmly. He spoke a little English and took delight in displaying his skill: "Very few strangers come to this restaurant." "It is one of the best restaurants in town." "I am an honest businessman."

Wine was the only drink available and two bottles were provided by our host, free of charge. It was pretty horrible stuff, but after the first few sips it seemed to improve. The menu was brought to us, clearly itemised and priced. Wishing to sample as many Mexican delights as possible, we chose carefully, a five-course meal being well within our monetary means. We ordered.

We waited. The wine tasted much better, so we ordered another two bottles. Our food would take some time, our host announced, but we didn't mind. We waited. Eventually our food arrived.

Each plate held six or seven small heaps of a reddish-brown glutinous mixture. It was hot and rather tasteless, but this was Mexico and this was what we had come for. We ate what we could. Perhaps the food was like the wine and would improve with each course.

We waited. We drank our wine. We waited. Eventually our hunger pangs began to get serious and we called on our host to bring the next course.

"More wine? You want more wine?"

"No. We want food. The next course please."

He didn't understand. We tried sign language. He still didn't understand. We tried to keep our tempers. "But there is no more," our host pronounced, "That is all you ordered."

We couldn't believe it: five courses all on that little plate. After a short conference between ourselves, we decided that enough was enough. Severe hunger pains had set in so we asked for the bill.

If the food was a shock, the bill was an even greater one. For six plates containing a few small dollops of inedible rubbish and four bottles of unpalatable wine, we were being charged the equivalent of £45, in 1968 a small fortune.

We remonstrated, but by now our amiable host was unable to recall even the most elementary English. His jolly face turned black with rage and he looked more and more like a Mexican bandit from the pages of a popular comic book.

One of our group was elected to act as negotiator. We were willing to pay for the wine and the meal, but a reasonable amount only. This was daylight robbery and paid no resemblance to the prices on the menu, which curiously, was now nowhere to be seen.

Our spokesman was calm and reasonable, even in the face of the fury of the restauranteur, who by now was screaming at the top of his voice. The word "Polizia" we recognised several times, and not wishing a brush with the law, we offered to pay two-thirds of the bill. This wasn't acceptable however, and next thing the screaming of sirens and the screech of tyres heralded the arrival of the Militia.

Four men in khaki entered the restaurant, each pointing a large pistol in our direction. They looked as if they meant business. The restaurant doors were clanged shut and locked. We were trapped!

The restauranteur now began a long speech, no doubt accusing us of much more than refusing to pay his inflated prices. I was petrified. None of our party looked too happy. I tried not to picture the inside of a Mexican jail, but the image kept appearing nonetheless.

The militiamen listened patiently to the restauranteur's long harangue. They were in no mood for arguing. The biggest and ugliest of the bunch pointed his gun to the final figure on the bill and held out his hand for the money. We paid up.

You would think we'd had enough excitement for one night, but we weren't ready to return to the ship. For a start we were very hungry. Secondly, we were all pretty merry, having consumed four bottles of wine between the six of us. We took a taxi to the best hotel in town, the Acapulco Princess.

"When the drink is in, the wit is out" is a saying my mother was wont to use, and it was certainly the case that night in Acapulco. As we draped ourselves round the pool bar, all thought of food vanished. "Let's try tequila" someone suggested. A round of drinks was ordered, costing almost as much as the restaurant bill, but the Assistant Surgeon was paying. We were shown how to drink the fiery liquid, straight, with a pinch of salt.

It was a lovely night. A full moon was shining on the still waters of the bay where the city lights stretched into the distance. The company was good and all our cares faded into the ether.

After several tequilas, someone had the wit to look at the clock and we realised that we had missed the last boat back to the ship. A taxi was ordered and the driver told to drive with haste, something he did with relish. The taxi screeched up to the pier just as the boat containing the agents and the Customs staff drew up. We were lucky.

Contact was made with *Orsova* and the agent directed the skipper of the launch to ferry us out to the ship. As we drew up at the pontoon, we could see the Master at Arms waiting, pencil and notebook at the ready. He shook his head in disbelief as two senior officers, three officers and one rather sheepish telephonist boarded. Our rather bedraggled and by now sober group retired to someone's cabin and tea and a mountain of toast was ordered from the galley to help us repent at leisure.

Los Angeles was our next stop and I had a second visit to Disneyland. It was Dorothy's first visit but there was so much to see that I was able to visit several different attractions without repeating any from my first visit. One in particular I describe in my diary as it made a great impression on me. This was the Enchanted Tiki Room which featured a concert starring four parrots and various other birds who talked, sang and danced their way through a routine that was enchanting to watch and brought a smile to our faces.

I had a few hours off in San Francisco and I took a tour of the Muir Woods, part of California's Golden Gate National Park and home to towering redwood trees. I spent an hour wandering through and admiring the giant trees. It had been raining earlier and the smell of the damp earth, peat, fern and pine was heady.

The return journey to San Francisco was through Sausalito, an artists' colony directly across the bay from the city. We had a leisurely walk round some of the small shops and art galleries and had coffee in one of the outdoor cafes which sported a wonderful view of the bay.

Our next stop was Vancouver, which was clean, fresh and cold. There was crisp white frost on the roads and snow on the hills. By the time I'd completed my shift in the telephone exchange, there was only time for a quick dash to the shops followed by a coffee and some delicious strawberry tarts, before heading back to the ship for the afternoon departure. As we sailed down the Queen Charlotte Strait, the sun was setting on the snow-covered hills above Vancouver turning them a brilliant shade of pink.

We now had four days at sea before reaching Honolulu and the weather was awful: high seas, grey skies and strong winds. Only when we reached our destination on day five did the weather improve. I was one of the first ashore to join a tour to the Blowhole and Haunama Bay, a brilliant semi-circle of sand bordered by palm trees where the Elvis Presley film, "Blue Hawaii" was filmed. We were the only visitors there and it seemed a shame that such a beautiful place should be so neglected by both visitors and locals. I would have stayed much longer but our tour was carefully orchestrated and we were ushered on to the next venue. Twenty minutes was not nearly long enough to soak up the atmosphere and keep an eye open for Elvis! That evening Ros and I went ashore to Woolworth's for a hamburger. Woolworth's in Honolulu was nothing like Woolworth's at home in Inverness. The café was basic, but as soon as we sat down a waitress arrived with a jug of ice-cold water and two glasses, together with warm napkins to wipe our hands. Our burger was served without delay and it was enormous. Although the order was just for a burger, it was accompanied by a huge salad and a mountain of chips. Suitably sated, we then moved on to the Sheraton Hotel where we treated ourselves to a Blue Hawaii cocktail.

The next four days at sea saw us experience a mixed bag of weather. For two days we experienced strong trade winds which whipped up the sea and kept the passengers well away from the open decks. Quite a few of them were seasick and stayed in their cabins. On the next two days we were in the doldrums. We crossed the equator at two o'clock on the afternoon of the first day and for the next two days the atmosphere was hot and sticky and enervating to the extent that even walking short distances was avoided if possible.

We arrived in Pago Pago at 10am and Noreen and I were first off the ship. We caught the local bus to Amanave at the northern tip of the island, at a cost of twenty-five cents each way. The driver and his chatty friend kept us entertained with their running commentary on where we were going and what life on Pago Pago was like. We stopped at one point, and the chatty friend jumped out of the bus and picked a couple of flowers which he insisted Noreen and I put in our hair. The bus also stopped every time we passed a pretty girl, so that both the driver and his friend could "chat her up." Also on the bus was an elderly couple from the ship who told us that they always looked at what the crew did as they seemed to know the best places to explore.

When we reached Amanave, it was the end of the road and as far as the bus was able to go. The village consisted of several straw

Waiting for Elvis.

huts with animals tied up outside, but no obvious sign of life. The driver's friend however, knew otherwise, and a visit to one of the huts saw him return with a large machete. He climbed a palm tree using his knees, feet and hands, and used the machete to knock down some coconuts. He then hacked the top off each coconut and we were able to drink the cool fresh milk which was delicious and very refreshing. The scenery here was superb. There were huge rocks jutting out into the bay and these formed small secluded sandy inlets, perfect for picnics.

When we returned to Pago Pago, we met up with some other friends and caught a bus going to the bottom end of the island where the scenery surpassed even that of the top end. There were many small curved bays with golden sand and fringed with palm trees. We got off the bus and paddled in the sea which was HOT! The stones and the sand were far too hot to stand on and we risked burned feet. A lady offered us some bananas which were growing beside her house. We accepted them, but they were pretty green and they didn't taste very good.

Our next adventure was a trip on a cable-car up to the local Radio Station. It was a bit scary as it was very high and the machinery squeaked and squealed a bit. When the cable-car stopped at the highest point about half-way across the bay, I got a bit worried and had thoughts of spending the rest of the day there unless the authorities had a contingency plan for a rescue. The cables looked as if they hadn't been serviced for many a long year. The stoppage wasn't too long however, and when we got to the top it was worth all the worry as the view was superb. We then had to do the journey in reverse and it was a very relieved group that got back to the village safely.

We arrived in Suva at 8am to a welcome from the Fiji Army band. A trip in a glass-bottomed boat out to the reef was a wonderful experience and we saw hundreds and thousands of multi-coloured fish and dozens of varieties of coral. An interesting and knowledgeable tour guide made the trip all that more enjoyable. Next on the itinerary was a trip to the Trade Winds Hotel where we enjoyed lunch, a cooling drink and a swim.

That evening, Frances and Dan MacLeod came on board and I was able to entertain them to drinks in the tourist lounge. It was on to the Trade Winds Hotel for dinner after which we sat by the pool and relaxed with a drink. It was a lovely balmy night with a full moon that shone on the calm, dark sea. We talked non-stop as Frances and Dan were keen to hear the latest news of Inverness. It was back to the MacLeod home for coffee then Dan ran me back to the ship for my spell on duty at midnight. I was very tired, but thankfully it was a quiet night.

I wasn't allowed to sleep next morning and was dragged ashore by Violet, Maggie P and Jacky for a stroll round the shops. Later I met Frances at the Travelodge Hotel for coffee. It was another hot day. Orsova sailed at 1pm and I stood on deck and watched the Fiji Police Band play us away from the quay. I then fell into my bed.

On my next visit to Noumea, four of us decided to spend some time at the beach. We were rather shocked when we bought four ice creams that cost us £2, a lot of money in 1973. The locals were beginning to realise there was money to be made from tourists. After my turn on duty in the afternoon, I went for a walk with two friends and they walked me off my feet. We sailed at seven and I was back on duty at nine. My diary says, "Thank goodness we're at sea tomorrow."

Climbing for coconuts.

After Noumea we hit some bad weather and were travelling very slowly. The vibration of the ship was bad and it kept putting me to sleep. The trouble wasn't entirely due to the weather and the engineers were working hard on solving the problem, but no mention was made to the passengers and when they commented on the state of the weather and the problems it was causing, no-one contradicted them.

Our next entertainment evening was Island Night and our group of eight dancers was performing the hula. We had been practising for a couple of weeks. We met in the Tourist Playroom at 9.30 pm for rum punch, and when we were all suitably relaxed and merry, we set off to meet up with the choir for the first of two performances, one in the First Class section and one in the Tourist Class section. The First Class ballroom was beautifully decorated. The entertainments staff had had a buying spree in some of the islands for suitable decorations and for our grass skirts and leis. Our dance was a great success and the atmosphere in the ballroom was electric. I enjoyed every minute.

After our first performance, we retired to the cabin of Allan where we relaxed with a drink and a sing-song before heading for the tourist section of the ship for the next performance. Our reception there was just as enthusiastic. We all got a bit carried away and managed to get some of the passengers to join us in our dance.

Being a member of the entertainment group meant that I was able to go on decks afterwards and mingle. This I did with gusto. I was getting bolder and my presence on the passenger decks was now being taken as normal. I aimed to keep it that way and was always aware that one false move and I'd be banished from the deck.

On our third day at sea we were getting restless. I organised a pour-out of mai-tais and we all got rather merry. I had to turf everyone out at 2.15pm however, as I was shampooing hair in the first class salon at 2.30pm. For our call at Melbourne next day, we had to place all our alcohol in bond. We were allowed to keep just enough for our use that evening and someone always organised a "dregs" party. Mona volunteered on this occasion and we all gathered at her cabin carrying our various bottles. The dregs never

Dancing the Hula.

seemed to run out however, as more and more kept arriving. We had a sing-song and a dance, then gate-crashed a party which was rather dull before we decided to call it a day and retire to bed.

Next day I visited Auckland Zoo. It was very hot, so we had a few ice-creams to cool ourselves down, at a more reasonable price than that paid in Noumea. It was still hot as we entered the Tasman Sea, but the crew were ordered into "blues" as the engine troubles were ongoing and the laundry was unable to generate enough hot water to launder the whites.

When we reached Melbourne, the tug operators were on strike and we couldn't manoeuvre into our berth unaided because of the wind. After standing offshore while we waited for the wind to abate, we managed to get into our berth and the passengers breathed a sigh of relief. They had had a couple of days of bad weather and were ready to experience dry land again.

Mona and I went ashore for lunch and a walk round the town centre. My spell on duty that afternoon was hard work as many passengers wanted to make phone calls and I was on my own. Luckily they were all very patient and I managed to get through a very busy four hours of non-stop activity with few problems. When I got off duty at 7pm Bob and Harold arrived at the cabin with pies and milk. They were both stoned, so Ros and I fed them the pies and made them milky coffee to sober them up then sent them on their way.

We arrived in Sydney at 9am and I was looking forward to seeing my brother Alistair and my sister-in-law Joyce who were living in Sydney while Alistair was on a two-year secondment to the Royal Australian Navy. They were living just upriver from Circular Quay in a flat rented from the Navy and it was nothing like service quarters in this country. The fourth-floor flat had a wonderful view of the Parramatta River and was tastefully furnished and fully equipped with every mod-con and gadget you could think of.

They arrived at the ship at 7.30pm. After a happy reunion, we headed to a lovely restaurant called Mother's Cellar for a meal. I spent the night at their flat where we talked non-stop catching up with all the news.

Next morning Alistair and I went shopping before picking Joyce up from work at 12.30. I had to work at 1pm but I arranged drinks and lunch on board for Alistair and Joyce and Deck Officer Bev Minter gave them a tour of the ship. I was off duty at 4pm when Ann Jack and her children arrived. Joyce had to work at 4pm but Alistair and Ann and family stayed for afternoon tea on board. We sailed at 7pm. I felt quite sad seeing Alistair standing on the quay waving. He had just enough time to drive round to the Sydney Harbour Bridge to see us sail under.

Two days later we were in Brisbane and Kay Summerfield and four children met the ship and took me out for the day. We had a wonderful tour of Brisbane then to Kay's house for lunch. She lived in Kenmore Drive, the next road along from Fortrose Street. I felt quite at home. Kay's husband Alistair joined us and they all came back to the ship where I gave them a guided tour and afternoon tea. Just after Kay and Alistair left at 5.30pm, Kay's mother and sister arrived for a tour of the ship and a drink. I was exhausted with all the talking and was glad when we sailed at 7pm.

We now had eight days at sea and had embarked a pilot to take us through the Great Barrier Reef and on to our next port, Singapore. The weather was hot and humid. The crew were in the throes of rehearsing for Olde Tyme Music Hall, with four shows in all, the first one in the crew quarters at 10pm. We'd had a curry lunch on one of the after decks for the birthday of Mike, one of the senior officers, so the final rehearsal didn't exactly go to plan.

The show itself that night was a riot and it was just as well it was the crew show. No-one was entirely sober, but we got through it without incident. I was singing "Burlington Bertie," dressed up in top hat and tails. What a wonderful feeling it was to hear the applause and the cheering that followed my rendition. I was quite elated. As usual there was a pour-out before the show and a party and sing-song afterwards, but I was exhausted and chickened out at midnight.

Next night we did the show in the Tourist section of the ship. I was working until 8pm and had to rush to get ready for the 8.15pm start. The Tourist audience was not all that appreciative of our efforts, not helped by a few naughty jokes made by the act of Bev and Peter, in their sketch "At the Railway Station." Also, Stan, who was playing the spoons, discovered that someone had pasted paper on to his spoons making them almost inaudible. He had to halt his performance while he scraped the paper off and he wasn't too happy. The audience went into howls of laughter which didn't improve Stan's mood and he cut short his stint and went off in a huff. However, all our problems were forgotten afterwards at the after-show party in the Tourist Playroom.

The First Class passengers appreciated our efforts the following night when we put on two shows for them. The first house was a bit subdued and I fluffed my lines, but the second house audience was fantastic and joined in the singing with gusto. There was yet another after-show party in the tourist playroom but by this time everyone was a bit tired and it finished early.

My second visit to Singapore was wonderful. We arrived early morning and I stood on deck and watched us sail into the bay which was crammed with large ships waiting to discharge their cargo, and small boats that darted about in a state of frenzy. I'd never seen such a busy harbour. I went ashore with Mona and Maggie F at 9.30 and went shopping where I bought a few presents for home. I was on duty 1-4.30 and again 7-9 when I was standing in for one of the telephonists, but after that I went ashore with Mona, Noreen and Keith. We met up with a group of engineers at Raffles Hotel and after a few drinks there, we headed for the Singapore night life.

Our large group had a wonderful meal at Fatty's, one of the outdoor stalls cooking delicious Chinese food. None of the stalls looked all that clean but we weren't too bothered and it wasn't until I had to go to one of the indoor toilets that I realised just how dirty some of the places could be. I took another slug of my drink and hoped that the alcohol would sterilise all the germs I'd already ingested.

Next we headed for Bugis Street and that was an eye-opener. We were a party of twelve, nine men and three women. Bugis Street was where all the transvestites hung out and they were out in their droves that night. No doubt they did a lot of business with the ship's crews. Several of these beautiful "lady-boys" descended on our table and proceeded to charm the engineers. The boys were all pretty merry and were not averse to a bit of chit-chat with the "girls". And these "girls" were beautiful. Apparently some of them have sex-change ops, but it would appear that their business on the streets of Singapore is temporary and as soon as they lose their good looks they go back to the Philippines, which, I was told, is where most of them originated, and back to the poverty from which they came.

The three girls had a rough time of it from the lady-boys. They obviously wanted rid of us. They maybe thought we were a hindrance to their attempts to seduce the boys and they were relent-

Singing Burlington Bertie.

less in their assault on us. They pulled our hair, nipped our skin, kicked our shins and even punched us when they got the chance. I was black and blue next day. Nonetheless, I found them fascinating and couldn't take my eyes off them. I tried to engage one or two of them in conversation, but they weren't interested. No doubt their livelihood depended on seducing some drunken sailor with a bit of money in his pocket. For me it was a night to remember and it was 3am before we dragged ourselves away and got back to the ship in a fleet of bicycle taxis. We sailed from Singapore at 6 o'clock that morning.

Three days at sea followed and the entertainment by the officers and crew carried on relentlessly. This time it was Oriental Night and I was taking part in a Coal-Miners' dance. It was rather slow and not very exciting, but the passengers enjoyed it and it got me up on deck for the evening. We celebrated in the Caribbean bar afterwards with champagne.

My one and only visit to Ceylon was four days later. I went ashore with Noreen and Mona and we went shopping for sapphires, having been told that Ceylon sapphires were the best in the world. I bought one for £11 and had it made into a ring when I got back home. We took a taxi to the Mount Lavinia Hotel where we had a curry lunch. The dining room looked out on to a long stretch of silvery sand with huge rollers pounding relentlessly on the shore.

I loved Colombo. There wasn't a lot of traffic on the streets and any traffic there was, consisted of bicycles and bullock carts. Everything about the town was quiet and relaxed and time seemed to pass slowly. People were keen however, to talk politics and they weren't too happy with the situation at that time.

According to one shopkeeper I got into conversation with, Mrs Banderanaika, the Prime Minister, was apparently in the hands of the communists who were taking over and slowly throttling the country. There were very few things imported. They hadn't tasted cheese or apples for three years. In the hospitals there were no drugs, so if you became ill, you died. Most of the shops were government-owned, or owned by some government official, so all the money went to the government or the rich officials, and the ordinary people lived at starvation level. We took a bag of apples ashore and gave them away, to the shop assistant, the waiter in the hotel, the taxi driver. They were all delighted.

The weather crossing the Indian Ocean was extremely hot for a change and I spent a lot of time on deck, in the shade, as my fair skin was apt to burn easily. I saw several fiery sunsets. I used to play a game with myself: every morning I'd try to pinpoint the exact spot where the sun would make its appearance. Watching the morning sky, navy blue, turning to purple, to red, to orange, and finally the moment when the sun burst over the horizon, was something that gave me great pleasure.

One morning I saw the Green Flash. Just as the tip of the sun peeped over the rim of the sea, a brilliant emerald flash stretched across the horizon. I was so stunned I cried out loud. Every night for about a week, the passengers had been lining the decks at sunset, hoping for a sight of this very phenomenon and being disappointed every time. I felt very privileged.

The Green Flash, which occurs at sunset but can also occur at sunrise, is caused by light refracting in the atmosphere. According to the website, *livescience.com*, what we are seeing is part of the sun suddenly and briefly changing colour. It lasts for a fraction of a second, which is why it is known as the Green Flash.

When we organised another Casino Night prior to our reaching Durban, it wasn't all that successful. The passengers weren't big spenders. On this leg from Sydney to Southampton, many of the passengers were young Australians. It was a rite of passage for many of them to spend a year or two working in the UK. London was full of them apparently. They may not have been big spenders but they knew how to enjoy themselves and the ship was a much livelier place for a few weeks.

Durban was another two-day stop. I wasn't able to go ashore on our arrival day as I had to work, but next morning I was up at the crack of dawn and went off on a tour to the Valley of a Thousand Hills. I don't remember much about the trip but I do remember the display of African native dancing where the female dancers were all bare from the waist up. My companion Bev was great company and we had a good giggle, especially at the bare-breasted dancers. We ordered milk shakes and cream scones in the café afterwards and discovered too late that we would probably have to wash the

Dancing the Can-Can.

dishes as we had trouble scraping enough money between us to pay for it.

Cape Town, our next stop was a short day call and as I was working all morning I only had a couple of hours ashore in the afternoon when I went shopping, a favourite pastime.

We now had seven days at sea before our next port, Dakar. My diary is blank for four of these days so I suspect nothing much happened. The crew were all getting a bit weary and looking forward to getting home. I do mention however, the atmosphere one day as we were coming up the west coast of Africa. It was cloudy with not a breath of wind and I mentioned that it felt quite eerie and brought on thoughts of The Ancient Mariner! Luckily there were no albatrosses about that day.

A letter written to my mother at about this time mentions that our troubles on board were far from over: "We've got seven cases of infectious hepatitis – six engineers and a waiter." This news was being kept from the passengers, but the crew knew all about it and were getting angry. My letter continues: "You should see the state

Relaxing with admirers and champagne.

of the galley – it is filthy. I'm surprised we haven't had something much worse. Something is being done at last, and last night I saw several of the deck crew hosing down the galley. It looks a lot cleaner today. It's a pity it has to take the signs of an epidemic before anything gets done."

The next entertainment night was a fashion show and by now I had graduated from being wardrobe mistress to model! I modelled a fancy nightdress belonging to Noreen and a striking black and white dress I'd bought in San Francisco. When I walked on wearing my dress there was an audible "Oh!" from the audience. I think they liked it.

I found another job on board to add to the other activities I carried out: that of ship's seamstress. The Officers had all been issued with new stripes and badges and when word got round that I was willing to sew them on and make holes and buttonholes in their mess jackets, I was inundated with requests, which kept me busy for quite some time.

During the next eight days at sea, I was part of a group of girls practising the Can-Can. We held our rehearsals in the Tourist play-room and these practice sessions were hilarious as there was always someone who would turn the wrong way causing a colli-sion which resulted in a heap of giggling bodies on the floor. We were also busy making our can-can skirts from material the host-ess had bought in Cape Town.

Our first performance was in the first class section of the ship. I wrote in my diary that we all went to the birthday party of one of the engineers beforehand, so we would have been relaxed and maybe not exactly sober when we danced, which would account for the comment in my diary: "we were a bit out of step but it wasn't too noticeable". After both shows we were feted by several of the elderly men on board who bought us champagne and want-ed to have their photos taken with us. We had six bottles of cham-pagne in total: two in first class, three in Tourist Class and one from the captain. I had to go on duty at midnight, and for the first (and last!) time I nodded off and slept through the buzzer when a call came in. It just happened to be the Purser, but I explained that I was busy and my excuse was accepted.

When we reached Dakar, Noreen and I joined one of the tours, but unfortunately I didn't record where we went or what we saw. I only say that I enjoyed it very much. In the evening I went to Violet's farewell party as she was leaving the ship when we got to Southampton. There were many farewell parties during the next few days and I had to pace myself as I still hadn't developed the stamina for prolonged partying.

Lisbon was our last port before Southampton and I stayed on board all day as I was feeling a wee bit delicate. I was on duty 9pm to midnight and worked on until 2am for one of the telephonists so that she could go ashore.

It was an early docking in Southampton and I was up early to organise the hire of a car as I was taking Ros home to Devizes before travelling up to Bristol for two days with my friend Gill. Two days later, on Friday 13th, I had another early rise and drove back to Southampton arriving at 11am just as the ship was in the middle of a Boat Drill. The medical staff, shivering on deck, gave a huge cheer as I showed off my driving skills with a fast and fancy manoeuvre and a sudden stop right at the bottom of the gangway.

We sailed at 1pm next day. We were heading for a series of cruises in the Mediterranean.

Part 10

The Final Voyage

April 1973 to June 1973

Our ship was visiting some of the ports for a second or third time, but I always found something new to see. Malaga was our first port of call where we were berthed next to General Franco's private yacht which was bristling with armed guards both on the yacht and on the quay. The surrounding area was also heavily guarded, with guns peeping from the roofs of all the flats overlooking the harbour. Franco spent about an hour strolling round the deck of his yacht under the watchful eyes of a couple of armed bodyguards who followed him everywhere, never leaving more than a couple of yards between him and them.

I joined a tour to Mijas which was a quaint little town of cobbled streets, whitewashed houses and spectacular views. The village was high up a mountain and was reached by a narrow road with rocks on one side and a sheer drop on the other. My heart was in my mouth more than once as we negotiated narrow bends and tricky passing-places.

In the evening a group of us went ashore in Malaga for paella and wine and were lucky enough to come upon a parade, a band of slow-marching soldiers, followed by a float of Christ on the Cross carried by about fifty or more men in uniform. In between the rows of soldiers, were hooded figures, dressed similar to the Ku Klux Klan, with only their eyes visible. They were carrying candles and looked rather sinister. We didn't have a very good view of the parade as we were at the back of a crowd that was about ten or twelve deep, but I chatted up a member of the Guarda Civil and he led us to the front of the crowd where we had a grandstand view of all that was going on. We had a mad dash back to the ship in time for our 11pm sailing and made it with just ten minutes to spare.

Lanzarote was our next stop and I went on a tour of a very picturesque village called Yaiza. Yaiza nestled beneath the Fire Mountains within the Timanfaya National Park. The vast desolation of the lava fields made me feel I was travelling on the moon, but it was interesting to see that grapes were grown extensively on the lava fields and appeared to be thriving. Apparently the film "1984" was filmed there as the area looked similar to the surface of the moon.

When we arrived at the foothills of the Fire Mountains, we were given a demonstration of how hot the earth is in this area. A bundle of dry brush was placed under a stone and it caught fire immediately. Then a beaker of water was thrown down a small hole and was expelled immediately as a mini geyser.

We passed massive salt flats, salt being a major industry in Lanzarote in the sixties and seventies, when between forty and fifty-thousand tons of it were mined each year and exported all over the world. Now there is only one salt flat remaining in Lanzarote and it has been turned into a tourist attraction. When freezing became popular, the fishing industry, which used salt as a preserving agent, stopped using it and there was no longer a call for the product.

We wandered round the quaint cobbled streets of the centre of Yaiza, between fairly substantial houses which were apparently built by island businessmen who considered Yaiza a very desirable place to live. A local winery was next on our itinerary where we sampled the local wine, but I appear not to have been too impressed as I noted in my diary: "Not very tasty."

It was Easter weekend and all of Spain was on holiday, so our visit to Las Palmas next day wasn't very successful. Five of us, all female, took the local bus to Maspalomas, a resort in the south of the island about forty miles away. It was like England on Bank

Holiday Monday! The traffic stretched for miles and we crawled along at a slow pace, the bus journey taking far longer than normal. We realised we had no time to do any sightseeing and decided to hire a taxi to take us back to the ship. All we could get was a mini-bus. When we asked the driver for a price, he just said "No problem" and didn't seem too keen to tell us what it cost. No wonder. When we got to the ship he asked for 250 pesetas for what we were told was a 30 peseta journey. He was obviously taking advantage of five women and hadn't bargained on us being well travelled and used to dealing with chancers like him. We gave him 50 pesetas and told him to take it or leave it as that was all he was getting. He took it.

In the evening, a group of us went ashore for a meal. Once again there was a parade of goose-stepping soldiers and several floats, although I haven't described what they were and my memory fails me. We enjoyed mingling with the crowd and took our time strolling back to the ship for our 1am sailing.

A couple of days later we were in Madeira, one of my favourite ports. My friends and I caught the local bus to Camara de Lobos which was a favourite haunt of Winston Churchill and where he did a lot of painting. It was a quaint little village with cobbled streets and dozens of fishing boats in the harbour. The only thing we couldn't cope with was the smell. It was a mix of fish, rotting seaweed and goodness what else. It was a hot day and the smell was probably intensified by the heat.

We had a day and a half in Southampton this time and I was first down the gangway when we docked. When we reached Southampton, the priority for the girls always seemed to be shopping. We stocked up on toiletries and other bits and pieces as the selection on board was limited and usually over-priced. We also got a bit fed up of ship food and the odd tin of baked beans sometimes found its way into the shopping basket.

Sailing day and we had a BBC film crew on board filming "Owen MD." It turned out that we didn't see much of them. They did their filming on deck and in the public rooms then disappeared to their cabins.

Two days later we were in Lisbon again and a group of us went ashore for a meal where we were given a whole chicken each! You might wonder why, when food on cruise ships is so good, that the crew took every opportunity in port to eat ashore. Mostly it was because we enjoyed the atmosphere of a foreign port. We always tried to eat at the places the locals used, rather than the establishments catering for foreign tourists. There the food was traditional and tasty and the prices reasonable. The locals always welcomed us wherever we went and enjoyed chatting to us in their limited English. Also, we could relax away from the strictures of the ship.

We arrived in Pyraeus at 1pm and Maggie Farmer and I got the train to Athens and a bus to Daphne. We walked round the 11th century Byzantine Monastery and had the place almost to ourselves. It was a magnificent building and the inside was cool and calming. The outside however, was clothed in scaffolding as it was obviously undergoing repair and restoration. We sat in the warm sunshine in the cloisters for quite some time before getting the bus and the train back to the ship.

Next morning Cristiana Kat and I went into Athens and found a long narrow street which was hosting a market. Street musicians, including a man with a barrel-organ, were playing enthusiastically to the crowds. We followed a narrow winding route up to the Acropolis and spent quite some time there drinking in the history and letting the mind wander back to ancient times. In 1973 visitors could still clamber over the Parthenon, but it is now closed off and has to be viewed from behind a barrier. We wandered through the massive pillars and sat on the steps enjoying the view of the city stretching out below. There were no crowds that day to spoil the atmosphere. It was very quiet. We stayed a bit too long however, and had to get a taxi back to the ship in time for sailing. We made it with minutes to spare.

Next day we were in Corfu. Maggie Farmer, Mona and I got a taxi to Achilleion where we visited the Achilleion Palace, built by Empress Elisabeth of Austria. It was a marvellous building, recently restored after being abandoned after the death of Empress Elisabeth and being damaged by invaders during both world wars. The villages of Gastourie and Benitses were also on our itinerary and we found Benitses especially picturesque with white-washed houses, narrow streets and smiling friendly people.

Next day we were at sea and for the first time I was invited for drinks in the Purser's cabin. A new purser had been appointed to *Orsova* and he was much more friendly towards the telephonists. He didn't seem to mind when I popped up at pour-outs and functions which were normally out-of-bounds to crew. It was in the purser's cabin that I met a couple from Invergordon: Mr and Mrs MacGregor who owned several shops in the town. Later in the week I was invited for drinks in their cabin and found myself in the company once again of all the senior officers. By now I believed I was one of them and I felt quite at home!

We had a twelve-hour turnaround this time in Southampton and it was difficult. I had a sore throat and felt quite ill so I didn't even go ashore but stayed in bed. The dispenser advised me to sleep between the blankets, not between the sheets and I perspired profusely and had to change my nightie twice during the night. I felt a lot better in the morning.

After a stop in Vigo, we had five days crossing the Atlantic when we experienced rough weather every day. Many of the passengers were seasick and the Captain's cocktail party had to be cancelled.

Barbados was our next port of call and we had two days there. I walked into the town in the morning but all the shops were closed. It was hot and the town was a wee bit smelly, so I simply walked back to the ship. In the evening, Noreen, Gill and I took a taxi to the Paradise Beach Hotel where we sat on the beach, drank Planter's Punch and listened to a steel band. It was a soft sultry night, just perfect. We paddled in the sea and walked on the warm sand.

Next morning I had to work 6-9 then three of us took a taxi to the Sandy Lane Hotel where we had coffee and a swim. We were joined at 1pm by Maggie Farmer who brought picnic lunches for us. We sat on the sand, sunbathed, strolled along the beach and paddled in the warm sea. We had the beach to ourselves.

We sailed at 5pm and later that night we held Caribbean Night on board and once again I was dancing for the entertainment of the passengers. That night we danced the Hukilau. Hukilau is a way of fishing invented by the ancient Hawaiians, where a large group of people work together in casting the net from the shore, then pulling it back. The dance mimicked the fishing ritual with long, slow, swaying movements simulating the throwing and pulling back of the net. It was a slow and relaxing dance and we enjoyed it. Also, we didn't make any mistakes. That didn't mean however, that everyone was completely sober. Prior to the first show we all met up in the Tourist Playroom for rum punch. After the first show we returned to the playroom for a second round of rum punch, and after the second show we retired to the Caribbean Bar where we tried to dance the limbo.

The limbo is a traditional dance contest which originated in the island of Trinidad and was usually an event that took place at wakes. A horizontal bar, the limbo bar, is placed on top of two vertical bars. The contestants try to go under the bar with their knees bent and their backs facing the floor. No part of the body must touch the bar and no part, other than the feet, must touch the ground. When a contestant knocks over the bar or falls, they are eliminated. When everyone has completed a turn, the bar is lowered and the contest continues. This goes on until the last contestant successfully limbos under the bar. Not many of us managed more than two or three rounds.

Next day we were in Grenada. After I finished duty at 1pm I went on a tour of the island by taxi. I was accompanied by three elderly passengers who, I write in my diary, were "a pain in the neck."

Grenada is an island country and consists of one largish island also called Grenada, and several smaller islands. The islands are known as The Spice Islands because of the numerous nutmeg plantations, the main product of the islands. We visited one such plantation where nutmeg was grown on a commercial basis and exported all over the world. The capital, St George's, was a compact little town consisting of colourful houses, Georgian buildings and a small, narrow harbour. French seemed to be the preferred language, but there was no problem ordering our coffee in one of the many outdoor cafes beside the picturesque harbour.

Martinique was our next stop and with three ports in three days, I was definitely flagging. I had three hours between shifts on duty and just had time to walk round the steep hills and narrow streets of Fort-de-France with its many small shops and cafes, and relax with a cold drink.

Martinique is an island that is part of the Lesser Antilles. It is mountainous and crowned by Mont Pelée, the volcano that wiped out the city of St Pierre in 1902. As an overseas region of France, this was reflected in the town of Fort-de-France, where French was the dominant language, although the atmosphere also had a West Indian feel to it.

Antigua was next and we docked at 7am. Along with six friends I left the ship early to spend a day on St John's beach. On the way, we heard loud bangs which the taxi driver told us were gun shots. Apparently there were riots in the centre of town and the taxi driver had to make a detour to avoid the area. We decided to carry on with our plans however, and spent several hours on the huge deserted beach, swimming and sunbathing and running along the sand. When our taxi arrived to take us back to the ship, the taxi driver informed us that there had been an attempted coup that morning, but it was all over and things were now back to normal. When we arrived back on board, we discovered that some of the tours had been cancelled because of the trouble and passengers and crew were advised not to venture into the town of St Johns. We were lucky to have gone ashore before the trouble started.

It was in Antigua that I received a letter from P&O headquarters saying that I was to be interviewed in Southampton when I returned there, for a post as hostess which I had applied for. I would be leaving the ship at the end of this cruise and several friends came to the cabin before dinner that night to help me celebrate by drinking a couple of bottles of champagne.

Next night we had another two houses of Olde Tyme Music Hall and I did my spot as Burlington Bertie again. I've written in my diary that the audiences at both houses were very wooden: not a chuckle or a smile, and we retired to the after-show party in the playroom to drown our sorrows. I couldn't drink too much as I was on duty at midnight and it was more than my job was worth to be unable to do it.

My last port was Madeira. Unfortunately it was a short stay of just six hours and I had to work four of them. I managed half an hour on the quay. In the evening Noreen hosted my farewell pour-out in her cabin. So many people came that Noreen had to impose a quick turn-around as there wasn't enough space in the cabin for everyone.

On the beach in Antigua.

Continental night followed and the girls did the Can-Can again in the two venues, but there was a dearth of champagne on this cruise and we had to buy our own. Once again I was on duty at midnight covering for one of the girls who had done a shift for me a few weeks before.

Three days before reaching Southampton on my final trip on *Orsova*, I recorded in my diary: "very busy day on duty as we have a waiter missing." This was another incident of homosexual misconduct, but as I didn't commit the details to paper, I am quoting from memory only. It was not the sort of incident I would tell my mother about so it didn't feature in any letters.

We had a young waiter who was on his first voyage with P&O. I believe he was married with a young baby. One night one of the galley staff invited him to his cabin for a drink, got the lad very drunk and sexually assaulted him. When the waiter woke up in the morning and realised what had happened to him, he threw himself overboard. The staff member was taken into custody until the ship reached Southampton where he was arrested by police and charged with manslaughter. I don't know what the result of this case was. I searched the newspaper archives online but was unable to find any reference to the incident.

When we reached Southampton, I did my last turn of duty on the switchboard from 6am till 9am. Next day I had an informal interview with the Entertainments Director regarding my application for a job as hostess. He told me that I would be called for a formal interview, but it wouldn't be for some months. In the meantime I should find a job in the entertainment business that would give me the experience I needed for the job at sea. I went home jubilant, knowing that I'd be back – sometime.

Epilogue

When I got home I started looking for jobs in the entertainment business. There wasn't a lot on offer. I contacted the Aviemore Centre, a sports and entertainments complex in the village of Aviemore, thirty miles south of Inverness.

The Entertainments Manager told me he had a vacancy for someone to organise the pony trekking and there could be a vacancy for a receptionist in the information bureau. Neither was what I was looking for, but as there was nothing else, I agreed to attend for interview.

The interview was easy. I liked Mr Johnston, the Entertainments Manager and thought we'd get on well. I wasn't told what position I was getting, until I started work the following Monday. When I was being taken round the various departments, to my astonishment, I was introduced by Mr Johnston as "my new secretary." I knew nothing about secretarial work and I certainly couldn't "take a letter" but I thought I might as well give it a go.

The job turned out to be much more interesting than I anticipated. Mr Johnston put me in charge of the reception staff and the cleaners, as he had problems controlling them, so he said. I was also involved with the running of the cinema, which had showings every afternoon and evening. There were two function rooms, one hosting a disco five nights a week and the other holding concerts or variety shows, folk nights and Scottish Nights when we attracted some well-known Scottish entertainers.

When the celebrities came to the Centre, Mr Johnston put me in charge of their welfare: making sure they were happy with their accommodation, had everything they needed and ensuring they got to the venue on time. Some were a bit difficult, but I enjoyed the challenge. I worked hard, putting in far more hours than my contract demanded.

I had been in my new job for about nine months when I was invited to P&O headquarters in London for an interview for the post of hostess. My slot was 11am. and I arrived early and took a seat in a small anteroom. The interviews were already in progress. Eleven o'clock came and went and I noticed that some girls were arriving after me but were being interviewed before me and I was beginning to think that I'd been forgotten. There was no-one around to ask. Eventually, several hours past my appointment time, I was called.

It was not a good interview. I was already out of my comfort zone and the waiting had added to my stressful state. The interview panel of three appeared to concentrate their questions on how I would fit into shipboard life as an officer after being a member of the crew. Would it be awkward for me? Would I be able to cope if I faced problems from crew or officers because of this? This line of questioning completely flummoxed me. The panel said they'd be in touch.

Three months later, I still had not had any communication from P&O so I gave them a ring. "No, you haven't got a job as hostess" I was told. "Did we not write to you?" Of course they hadn't. I wasn't too pleased.

Luckily my disappointment was tempered by the fact that I was thoroughly enjoying my job at the Aviemore Centre. I was getting more responsibility. Assistant Managers tended not to stay very long, so I was given more and more of their work. I forgot about P&O.

I didn't lose touch however, with the friends I'd made at sea, and over the years several of them came to stay with me in Aviemore and Rosemarkie. I also visited them fairly regularly.

This contact continues. I'm an Associate Member of POMS, the P&O Medical Society. The group consists of doctors, nurses, dispensers and "hangers-on" like me, who have been invited to join as Associate Members. We meet at least once a year and in 2017 the society celebrated twenty years of existence. It's a great way of keeping in touch with my old ship-mates and meeting new ones and this annual meeting is a highlight in my calendar.

POMS reunion in Menorca 2015.

Acknowledgements

When I was clearing my loft a few years ago, I found a cardboard box labelled "P&O" which contained a mass of papers, booklets, receipts, diaries and crucially, all the letters written to my mother during my time working for P&O on board ship. These letters and diaries are the basis of the contents of this book. I was an inveterate note-taker when I was at sea, and made notes of every conversation and incident, every view and action worthy of comment, which were then incorporated into the long newsy letters I wrote home. Nothing was too trivial to report, so my notes and letters contain long-forgotten incidents and descriptions of places vastly altered in the intervening fifty years.

Information on the ports visited, was taken initially from the P&O port notes which were issued to passengers at every port. This has been supplemented by accessing the various on-line history sites and tourist information sites for each of the ports. Wikipedia was also a good source of the current situation in the cities and ports visited by P&O.

The photos come from several sources. Most of them are mine, but the on-board activities were official photos taken by the ship's photographer. Two photos I have taken from the site "Old Seadogs Reunited." I tried several times to contact the site to request permission to print the photos but got no reply. I have taken the liberty of using the photos and attributing them to the Old Seadogs site.

My thanks are due to several people who answered questions when my notes and my memory let me down, or supplied information on the current situation concerning life on board a P&O liner. Identification of faces of people last seen fifty years ago, proved difficult as the memory of some of my seagoing friends was just as bad as mine, but Alison Ross, Maggie Lumb (nee Farmer), Violet Jardine, Janice Harris (nee Shingleton) and Rory Smith came up trumps.

Elizabeth Sutherland and Sheena Munro read my script with a view to identifying grammar and typing errors and Violet Jardine made sure I didn't have any P&O errors. My thanks are due to them all and any others I may have missed.